Increasing Confidence

First published 2021

Published under licence by Brown Dog Books and
The Self-Publishing Partnership, 7 Green Park Station, Bath BA1 1JB

www.selfpublishingpartnership.co.uk

ISBN printed book: 978-1-83952-258-1
ISBN e-book: 978-1-83952-259-8

Cover design by Kevin Rylands
Internal design by Andrew Easton

Printed and bound in the UK

This book is printed on FSC certified paper

MIX
Paper from responsible sources
FSC® C013604

A Practical Guide to Increasing Confidence

Written by **Charlie Wardle**

HEALTH & WELLBEING

CLIMB YOUR MOUNTAIN

Table of Contents

Introduction

'The greatest journeys all start with a single step... often you can't see the top of the mountain when you set off on your climb. With every step you gain experience, perspective, skill, confidence and motivation to help you towards achieving your goal.'

I have written this book with the aim that you, the reader, can increase your confidence and motivation so you will achieve more, which in turn will further increase your confidence and motivation and help you lead a happier and healthier life. We all want to be happy and healthy, yet the reality is that many of us are not and I want to play a small part in improving people's lives.

Through my own experiences, good and bad, years of reading, research, meeting people, gaining knowledge and understanding of what works and what doesn't, I believe this book can help you become happier and healthier by focusing on the three areas of confidence, motivation and achievement.

As I have said in my other books, there is no magic wand, and it does take time, effort and patience to get the desired results and rewards, but always remember that those results and rewards are worth it. I have tried to make the book straightforward to read and go through and I really hope it will make a positive difference to your life and I wish you all the best.

Please also look at the section of the book with more information about the Climb Your Mountain charity and how you could further benefit or help us so we can continue to help more people. The website for the charity is **www.climbyourmountain.org** and there is also a donation page on there as well as details of the other books, the well-being walks, the health and well-being talks, the fundraising challenges and how to volunteer.

Coronavirus impact

I don't know when you are reading the book but I am writing this in November 2020 and in England we are currently going through another, albeit shorter and slightly less restrictive, lockdown. I think it is fair to say that in early 2020, nobody could have imagined how 2020 would have turned out and how the Coronavirus would have had such an impact on our lives and for most people a very negative impact.

Although very recently we had news of a potentially successful vaccine to come, there has been and still is so much uncertainty on what will happen and when. Tens of thousands of people have lost their lives and many millions have had their lives completely thrown into turmoil and despair. Whether that be for financial reasons, their job, their livelihood, their social life, their relationships, their physical health, their mental and emotional well-being and many other factors, the pandemic has caused such issues for nearly everyone and for all ages.

Fortunately, this kind of enormous, life-changing-for-all event is rare but at the same time because it is rare it means that it is very difficult to deal with as the knowledge, understanding and experience is not there to help. Of course, terrible things happen all the time and have always happened but usually only a small minority of people are affected at any one time, yet with the Coronavirus, the impact has affected the vast majority of people, many of whom are encountering issues that they have never faced before.

Faced with such issues and such uncertainty, more people than ever are going to struggle with anxiety, depression, stress and a lack of confidence. There has been huge demand for the other books I've written on *Overcoming Anxiety* and *Beating Depression* and I hope this book will also be beneficial. Perhaps more so than ever, as we go through the

Coronavirus crisis and start to come out the other side, we need to gain knowledge and understanding of our mental and emotional health and find the motivation to increase our confidence so we can come through this stronger, more resilient and going forward become healthier and happier.

We need to look after ourselves, recognise issues, look out for others, show more empathy and put the effort in, as the alternative is an even worse prospect that nobody wants. We have to take responsibility and although it can be tough, there are significant gains and rewards that will come as a result of those efforts. So please make that effort, starting with reading this book, and things will improve.

I love this quote attributed to Mahatma Gandhi and I feel it is very relevant to today's situation, so as I've mentioned, there is no better time than now to do the things that are going to help you and others you care about, so go for it!

'Be the change you want to see in the world.'

CONFIDENCE

Why is confidence so important?

'A bird sitting on a tree is never afraid of the branch breaking, because its trust is not on the branch but on its own wings.'

Being confident is a wonderful thing for so many reasons and confidence plays a huge role in our lives. Confident people are happier, healthier, more motivated, more resilient and less prone to issues such as anxiety and depression. On the contrary, when your confidence is low, the opposite is true. So many people, unfortunately, lack confidence, which has a negative impact on their lives in many ways, yet the good news is, your confidence can be increased and the wide range of benefits this brings can be realised, both in the short and long term.

The reality is that the majority of people are low on confidence and even those with reasonable levels of confidence can still improve their lives significantly by increasing their confidence further. So this book is really designed for anybody who wants to increase their confidence and therefore have a happier and healthier life, and I strongly believe that if you read, understand, apply and practise, then that will happen and the rewards are so worth the effort.

Over many years I have studied, researched, read about and met thousands of people with anxiety and depression issues, which are common and are sadly increasing. However, my belief is that for the majority of these people the underlying issue is one of confidence, and the issues of anxiety and depression stem from a lack of confidence (usually throughout their life) and by focusing on increasing confidence, any issues of anxiety and depression will be greatly improved as a result. Understanding what confidence is and how confident (or not) you are, is fundamental to your mental health, happiness and overall health.

However, it's important to remember that there is no magic confidence wand. Your confidence can and will increase but it will take time and effort and there are many aspects to confidence that need to be recognised and understood. The book aims to cover all these different aspects in a straightforward and practical way to make it easier, but ultimately you are responsible for reading, understanding, applying and practising everything and as I have previously said above, it is worth it!

'Men often become what they believe themselves to be. If I believe I cannot do something, it makes me incapable of doing it. When I believe I can, I acquire the ability to do it even if I didn't have it in the beginning.'

Mahatma Gandhi

What is confidence?

Confidence – *The anticipation of a positive outcome; and if the outcome is not positive, knowing you can deal with it!*

Before you embark upon your increasing-confidence journey, it is important to first understand what I mean by 'confidence', what you mean by 'confidence', and what the rest of the world means by 'confidence'. These definitions can all differ greatly and it is vital that you understand exactly what it is you want to develop before you start working to develop it.

Our confidence levels affect us in our daily lives in all kinds of ways. They affect our work, relationships, friendships, fitness, health, thinking, beliefs, actions, attitudes, behaviours, happiness... The list goes on.

The vast majority of people would like to be more confident and certainly nobody would want to feel less confident than they do. So if most people want to be more confident, that would imply there is an issue that really should be addressed.

In order to develop your own confidence you need to understand confidence, both the general understanding and also your own personal understanding, as this can often differ considerably. Your perception of confidence, your own and other people's, could be very different from how someone else sees it and what the main factors are related to your differing perspectives.

So we need to hear from different people, look at different factors, understand different elements and then bring these all together so that you have a much better understanding of confidence. Once you understand confidence you are then in a much better place to actually start building your own confidence and becoming a more confident and self-assured person.

I believe there is always an explanation for how someone behaves and thinks. The key is to try and understand the reasons behind those thoughts and actions. With regard to confidence, with this book you can work out why you don't feel confident and then look at how best to address these areas in the most effective way. We will look at what the key factors are and seek to put in place plans to overcome, prevent, discard, build upon, reframe, or change them.

This book helps you to understand confidence and gives you practical ways to improve your confidence using a range of tools, techniques and tips that should be practised and reinforced. The more you practise, the easier it becomes and the more confident you become.

'Whether you think you can or you can't, you will (most probably) be right.'
Henry Ford

I love this quote from Henry Ford. It is so true that your beliefs and thought processes are so important to the results you achieve in life. Your chances of success and getting the result you want are greatly improved if you think that will happen, and conversely the chances are greatly diminished if you think you can't achieve the results you want.

A recent example that highlights this for me was on a weekend group trip to Snowdon that I organised. It was a relatively small group that included a mix of new people and a few more experienced participants who had attended our trips before. I was introducing people to each other on the Saturday morning and one of the new ladies immediately said how she was hopeless with names and would never remember anyone. As people often do, she said it in a half-joking way and quickly repeated again how she could never remember people's names and was useless at that kind of thing.

Later in the day, I asked a few people in the group if they had remembered everyone's names and did a few quick tests at random. Once again, the same lady quickly said how she was rubbish with names and wouldn't be able to remember, claiming she had always been useless with names. We continued with the day but at dinner in the evening I was seated next to this lady and after a while I raised the subject of the names of other people in the group. Again she reiterated how bad she was with names, always had been and she was useless at anything like that.

I asked her if she would try, just for a couple of minutes, forgetting about how bad she was and instead believe she could do it and just focus on each member of the group. Within a few minutes she had remembered everyone's names and she was visibly quite shocked and surprised that she had done this.

For nearly all her life she had immediately put up a barrier with the belief she couldn't do this task. She had no confidence at all in her ability to remember names. She believed she wouldn't be able to remember, so she didn't. Most likely she had experienced something when she was younger that knocked her confidence in this way and made her feel like she couldn't do this or similar tasks. Also likely was that someone else had told her this was the case, and with absolute certainty she herself had reinforced this negative belief continually ever since.

This belief and attitude will only ever remain and become even more fixed if it is not addressed. However, it was proven within a few short minutes that she wasn't useless and she could remember the names with a little focus and effort. So going forward in any similar situation, her instinct needs to be that she can rather than she can't. This will require practice as such an ingrained belief can be difficult to change, but it can change and with that change a greater confidence can be gained.

No longer does she have to put up that barrier and hold that negative belief about herself. In so many cases people will have these false barriers and beliefs due to past experiences or people telling them they can't do something. The reality is that in many cases the person can, and when they think and believe they can, then they will!

Below are real answers from real people I asked the following questions of and that give you an insight and a wide range of views around the subject of confidence:

What is your definition of confidence?

- *Feeling self-assured – having self-belief and faith in yourself. Not questioning yourself all the time, not doubting yourself. Being established in life and feeling capable and competent.*

- *Not having 'the fear of failure' sitting on your shoulder. Being able to say what you feel/believe without the fear of being wrong or appearing idiotic.*
- *Being comfortable with who you are and resilient to negative influences. To be comfortable in your own skin and to be able to express yourself openly.*
- *Being able to talk or put forward your opinion on something to others in any given situation (i.e. in a one-on-one conversation, in a small group or on a much larger scale, say as part of a presentation or talk) without hesitation. Believing in yourself enough that you are sure of what you are saying and doing.*
- *I would describe it as the ability to project and feel good in yourself, with what you do and how you do it. Being assertive and able to get a point or opinion across. Not feeling awkward or lost.*
- *To me it's the ability to stand up for yourself and your beliefs, and the ability to make others believe them too.*
- *The ability to do things you want without worrying about what other people might think. Being happy with yourself and comfortable in who you are. Believing in yourself and your decisions.*

What are the characteristics/behaviours of a confident person?

- *Self-belief, no hesitancy with their own opinions, stop looking to others for reassurance, having individuality, being unafraid to walk alone (i.e. not follow the crowd).*
- *Characteristics are being positive, assertive, having self-belief and being happy with their abilities. Their behaviours are being able to communicate well with presentation skills, with a professional image*

and being able to take the lead.

- *Someone who is able to chat to others whatever the situation, who is not afraid to speak up and is able to say what they think in a convincing way or to get their point across clearly without sounding arrogant. Someone who doesn't care if they look stupid if they say or do something wrong.*
- *Open body language, holding their head up high, speaking clearly, maintaining eye contact with the person they're speaking to, relaxed shoulders and body posture.*
- *They appear sure of themselves and in their abilities. They may come across as bubbly or direct. They may be chatty and able to tackle new things more easily. I believe an inner belief in one's self would make a person more confident.*
- *Someone who is confident projects a high self-esteem, is happy to celebrate success and accept compliments, but equally is able to hold their hand up and admit a mistake and change course. Confident people are positive and transformational in their thinking; barriers are there to be overcome, not to block their way.*
- *They are happy and comfortable with themselves. They aren't concerned about what other people think about them, and they don't compare themselves to other people.*

What do you fear? What do you worry about?

- *Going out to work and holding it together. Not being able to get a job (contradictory with first item). Being found out to be incompetent/a fraud. Being tired. Beating myself up about my capabilities.*
- *Talking in a large group of people. Saying the wrong thing. Feeling stupid. Upsetting people. Worrying about what people think. Money and security.*

- *Looking like a fool in front of other people. Lack of control, being in a situation that's out of my comfort zone.*
- *I have quite a strong fear of social situations and interaction with others. Not a confident conversationalist. I hate having focus put on me, dislike even being on camera or hearing my own voice played back. I have always had a sense of being a bit 'odd' and not fitting in or belonging in groups of people so tend to withdraw when I'm feeling at my most vulnerable.*
- *Feeling pain emotionally, what other people think of me, making a mistake, failure, going into the unknown (networking, interviews, first-time situations), situations I can't control (flying).*
- *I fear change and I do not like to feel unsettled. Work causes me a lot of worry and makes me unhappy at times. What people think of me worries me; even if they say positive things about/to me I still doubt.*
- *Worry that someone wouldn't like me and that I can be socially awkward. Financial issues stopping me doing things I like. Putting on weight and feeling unattractive.*
- *I fear being unhappy. I worry about what will happen in my life, my job, relationships etc. I am worried that I am not making the most of my life. I also worry about bad things happening to my family and friends, illnesses, death etc.*

Why would you like to be more confident?

- *So I can be happy with myself and my life. I would like to be able to think more positively and not be so down about myself. Would also hopefully like to meet people who feel the same as me so I don't feel like the shy odd one out.*
- *I suppose I am mostly thinking on a personal level that I want to be able to open up to new people, to follow up meeting people with a*

phone call. My children will be leaving home in the next few years and I want to move into a new life phase with new aims.

- *I would like to get back the confidence I used to have because life was so much easier/better that way. I believe I will be much happier and accepting, I will stop worrying. I will get back the motivation and concentration to study and learn. I will clear my mind of all the things that I worry about now and I will focus on setting and achieving goals.*
- *I would like to be more confident in order to live my life in a happier and settled way with true belief in myself. Being less negative, I feel, would help me be more confident. I would like to find a belief in myself at these workshops and be able to explore what would make me more confident and happy. I would also like to stop the negativity that seems to have always been a big part of my life.*
- *I believe not feeling confident is actually affecting me physically and emotionally every day of my life and has done for many years. I want to feel better about myself and strong enough to go ahead and achieve some of the things I've always wanted to.*
- *I want to feel like I believe that people value what I say. I want to feel that I can make a difference. I want to learn new ideas and/or receive reinforcement of existing ideas that will enable/assist me in the process of validating my opinion/input.*
- *To gain inner confidence and self-belief in myself. To be able to sell myself in an interview to get a great job that I love. Not to worry so much about what people think.*

Know yourself

Your values, identity and integrity

Before going into more detail about understanding confidence it is essential that you consider your own values, identity and integrity, as they are fundamental to who you are, what you want from your life, how you deal with situations and how you react to people. Everyone is different and this is a result of nature, nurture, circumstances and experiences. Everyone will have their own values, identity and integrity as a result. These values are core to that individual and to be true to yourself you must stick with these values to maintain your own identity, integrity and beliefs. If you stray from these values, for whatever reason, then you are likely to feel worse about yourself and lose your integrity, and as a result your confidence could be affected.

'The greatness of a man is not in how much wealth he acquires, but in his integrity and his ability to affect those around him positively.'
Bob Marley

So take time to understand yourself and who you are. A great story that highlights this is from the most sacred place in the ancient world, the oracle at Delphi in central Greece. Kings, warriors and envoys travelled from across the known world to hear the prophecies of the oracle. Above the gates at Delphi, a short inscription greeted every weary traveller: ***Know thyself.*** This simple advice was considered the most important piece of knowledge anyone could possess. And to understand what the oracle told you, you first had to understand yourself.

You may find yourself in difficult positions, perhaps due to other people, financial issues, relationships, stress, depression, work problems, drink or drugs, where you find yourself compromising your own core values. Whether you want to admit to it or not, you will be aware, and the further away you stray from your core values the worse your situation is likely to become.

It is important that no matter what is happening in your life you can retain your values and integrity so that you are able to look yourself in the mirror and know that you are being true to yourself and true to your values. Life will always throw you curveballs; some people will always let you down, have a different view, misunderstand the situation etc., and there will always be some issues to deal with in life. We just need to teach ourselves how best to deal with these issues and challenges.

One of the best ways to understand your own core values is to ask yourself what matters most in your life, what are the most important things, and what characteristics in people do you respect the most? Take some time to really work out what is important to you and look to define and document these core values.

Something else that can be helpful is to think about a person, or people, whom you admire and respect the most – whether that is someone you know personally or perhaps a famous name you look up to. Then consider what it is about them that you really admire and respect. What is it about their behaviour, actions, words, achievements etc., that you hold in high regard? Maybe it's their courage, determination, resilience, honesty etc. It is quite likely that your core values and what you see as truly important are very similar to what you recognise, admire and respect in that other person.

Knowing the real you and having your own identity is really important in order to retain your values and integrity. Often people will lose their way, no longer sure of who they are, living a life for others rather than their own life and not feeling like the real them any more.

So spend time understanding the real you, knowing your core values, having your own identity and always maintaining your integrity. These are fundamental foundations for your health and happiness in general, and very specifically for your own self-confidence.

'It's not the mountain we conquer, but ourselves.'
Sir Edmund Hillary

Take responsibility

It is your life and you are responsible for it. Of course, there are many people in your life, past and present, that have an effect and also many other factors that have an impact, but it is essential that you are accountable and take personal responsibility for what you do in your life. The more responsibility you take, the more control you have over your own life and you are able to shape it in the way you want.

It is important to have help, directly or indirectly, but a good analogy is climbing a mountain. You may have guides on the climb, people advising beforehand on the best kit, preferred routes, dangers to look out for, weather conditions, etc., all to help you, but ultimately you are the one who has to walk, hike, climb and put one foot in front of the other to get to the summit. Nobody can do that for you and when you take responsibility for yourself, with help from others, you are more likely to succeed on the climb and the rewards from doing so are much better.

Internal vs. external thinking

As well as our negative or positive belief systems, we also have differing ways in our thinking in terms of whether it's internal or external. Again, there is a wide spectrum, from extremely internal to extremely external and everything in between, yet we will all fall somewhere within this range.

Generally speaking the more internal your thinking is then the more confident you will be and you will feel more powerful and be more in control of your life, which has to be a good thing. The more external your thinking is, the less in control you are. You will often feel powerless and lack confidence, which will generally have a negative impact on your life.

If a person has a strong internal way of thinking, they will believe that this can usually control or strongly influence their life in terms of their experiences and what will happen to them, and also be able to deal with anything that has happened to them. They feel more powerful, responsible and in control, and this thinking increases confidence.

On the other hand if a person has a strong external way of thinking then they will think that their life and experiences are more often than not controlled or strongly influenced by external factors such as other people, luck, fate, God, etc. This way of thinking is often disempowering and will most likely reduce confidence. They feel they don't have much control or influence over events, or their life in general, and everything happens to them as a result of outside factors and influences.

The more you can have an internal way of thinking and thus feel more powerful, more in control, more influential and more confident over your life and what happens, the better. It will significantly help in the fight to beat depression.

If you are relying on luck, or other people or some kind of greater being to come and rescue you and make your life wonderful then the chances are not much will change. If, on the other hand, you can become more internal in your thinking then you can have much more direct influence on your life and be more in control.

Make a real effort to dismiss anything that is external and instead focus on what you can do yourself to have more power and influence over your own life.

Examples of internal thinking and behaviours	Examples of external thinking and behaviours
I passed my driving test because I put in lots of practice and I really focused.	I don't know how I passed my driving test – it must have just been a lucky day and the examiner was feeling generous.
I didn't get that promotion at work but the other candidate was really good so I now know what I must do and work on so next time I will.	I didn't get that promotion at work. It's not fair and I'm always unlucky. There's no point even trying.
I need to try to get fitter so I'm going to enter a 5km event, set out a training plan, and then get going.	I need someone else to help me get fitter as I just can't get motivated and do it on my own.
I'm hiking up a mountain at the weekend and the weather forecast doesn't look good so I better make sure I have my waterproofs. It will be more of a challenge!	I'm hiking up a mountain at the weekend and it's just my luck that the weather forecast is rubbish. Why does this always happen to me? Well, I will cross my fingers and hope it won't rain too much.

'If we want to feel truly confident, we must break the habit of trying to please all people, all of the time.'

Gael Lindenfield

The Rocky technique!

I have a technique that I have used effectively when going through a really tough time, with things going wrong, bad news following more bad news, knock-backs, setbacks, people letting you down and life seemingly throwing a whole barrage of punches at you. I imagine I am in a boxing fight and life is my opponent, throwing all these punches at me. Life is in control, it is winning, it is hurting me and I can't seem to do anything about it... however, defence is so important to a boxer. Being able to defend the punches and onslaught is often more important than being able to throw punches yourself.

So my focus is on defending myself as best I can, staying strong, arms up, protecting myself. I realise that although uncomfortable and causing some pain, I can deal with it. Those punches are not going to knock me out, I can absorb them, soak them up and keep standing. Nothing life throws at me is going to put me down on the floor, my defence is strong and the longer these punches are thrown at me the stronger I feel, knowing they cannot hurt me. I am too resilient, my defence is too strong and this is my time to recover while life throws its punches and wears itself out. I can wait for now, with my defence strong and my confidence growing, and when the time is right it will be my turn to step forward and throw a few punches.

'You, me, or nobody is going to hit as hard as life. But it ain't about how hard you hit. It's about how hard you can get hit and keep moving forward. How much you can take and keep moving forward. That's how winning is done!'

Rocky Balboa

Resilience

Although at the time when struggling with things and when confidence is low it is very difficult to deal with, you should always try to remember that by going through these tough times you will build resilience and that in turn can build confidence and the ability to deal with things in the future. The saying ***'what doesn't kill you, makes you stronger'*** is very true and having more resilience is a great asset and can definitely help increase confidence.

Knowing that you have been through difficult situations, survived and come out the other side means that you are strong and can deal with these issues. Resilience gives you the ability to deal with future setbacks, problems, bad news, tough times etc. that will undoubtedly come, as that is the nature of life. Everyone goes through tough times, often when you least expect it, and having the experience of dealing with similar situations in the past should give you more confidence in your ability to deal with any new issues arising.

Always try to look at the positives in any situation and when times are tough, remember two things – firstly, you can deal with them and get through them as you have done previously, and secondly, it will build even greater resilience and more confidence for the future.

Be positive, productive and optimistic

You are more likely to feel confident if you are a hopeful and optimistic person, thinking forward more positively with a glass-half-full approach to life. If you are pessimistic, thinking the worst, being negative and often looking backwards then your confidence is likely to suffer as a result. Generally the more confident you are, the more optimistic and vice versa. Optimism is generally a state of mind over which you have some control. You can choose to be more optimistic and hopeful with your attitude and thus it makes sense that if you do this then your confidence is likely to increase. Think about the people in your life who make you happy, and distance yourself from those who don't – people who undermine you and your confidence, and belittle you, should have no room in your life.

- **Thinking positively**

Life will always throw stuff at us that we don't like, don't want to deal with, and don't want to happen and of course, life is not fair. However, by being pessimistic and negative, things will not improve and it will become harder to deal with life's challenges. By thinking positively and choosing to have that positive mindset you are making improvements to the situation. You are making a positive difference and even if that's all you are able to do, then choosing to think positively will be beneficial. Plus, the brain can only think one thought at a time, so make it a positive one!

- **Things to look forward to**

It is also really important to look forward positively and this will be helped by thinking of things that you will look forward to. Things that you wish to do, places to go, people to see, skills to learn, challenges to achieve etc., are all positive, forward-looking things that create an optimistic and hopeful mindset that in turn helps to boost confidence.

- **Things to smile about and feel good about**

It is great when we feel happy, feel good about things, and smile. So take opportunities to think about examples of what does make you smile and feel good. What events, people, activities, experiences have made you feel good? What and whom makes you smile? Think about how you can have more of these experiences and make the effort to do more things that will make you smile, that you will enjoy and feel good about. Look at photographs to reaffirm that you have had great times in your life. Holiday photos are always a pleasure to look at, and ones of you smiling, having fun and making memories are a positive boost to your confidence. The more you do, the more confident you will feel.

- **Hope is the best of things**

There is a quote from one of my favourite films (*The Shawshank Redemption*) that goes: 'Hope is a good thing, maybe the best of things, and no good thing ever dies.' It is important to remember this; no matter how low you may feel or how bad a situation you may go through, hope is always there and you need to hold on to that. Behind every dark cloud sits the sun, waiting to appear.

'Hope is a good thing, maybe the best of things, and no good thing ever dies.'

Positive affirmation exercises

One of the best ways to boost confidence is to spend time thinking about all the positive things in your life currently, the positives from the past and all the positive things you will be doing in the future. Positive thoughts are more likely to lead to positive actions, and positive actions will lead to increased confidence. And of course it is much more enjoyable to be in a positive mindset and have a positive mental attitude than a negative one.

The more you practise and make the effort to think positively, the easier it becomes, and more natural. It basically becomes a very productive and beneficial habit. It may feel odd at first or you may not feel like being positive but you do have the choice. You have the choice right now whether to focus on positives or negatives – so choose the right option!

Here are some things you can try to help with the positive thinking. It's not rocket science but it does work and can be really effective!

Each night as you lie in bed before going to sleep, spend a couple of minutes just thinking about the positives. Do not focus on anything negative. Only focus on the positives and keep reaffirming these examples.

Each morning as you wake up in bed, spend a couple of minutes just thinking about the day ahead with a positive attitude. Think about what you will do that is positive with specific examples. Have these positive thoughts in your head, then get out of bed enthusiastically with a can-do attitude knowing there will be lots of positives for you during the day ahead.

Keep repeating this each night and each morning. The more you practise this the easier it will become and the better the results. It only takes a few minutes so continue to make it part of your day – a great habit to have!

If you do get any **negative thoughts** in your head whilst doing these exercises then do your best to kick them into touch straight away. As soon as you notice anything negative, get rid of it and focus all your thoughts back on something positive. This will become much easier the more you practise.

Using this table may help to structure your thoughts, and I have included an example that might be helpful. Use the table to write down your own positive experiences (but don't limit them to just five!).

What is the positive experience?	For what reasons is it positive?	What praise would you give if someone else did this?	What can you learn from this experience?
E.g. I climbed Mount Snowdon	A healthy challenge, new experience, new scenery, pushed myself, met new people	Great achievement, shows determination and effort	I can do more than I think, great feeling of accomplishment, step out of comfort zone was good experience

Manage your chimp – be in control

A book that I would strongly recommend is ***The Chimp Paradox* by Dr Steve Peters**. He is best known for being the team psychiatrist for British Cycling and Team Sky, helping the likes of Sir Chris Hoy, Sir Bradley Wiggins and Victoria Pendleton. The book is described as a mind-management plan and tries to explain the different way the brain works based on neuroscience principles; this in turn helps explain the different thoughts and behaviours we have. By understanding why we think and behave in certain ways it is then possible to be more in control of our thoughts and behaviours in order to reduce any anxiety and increase our confidence, happiness and success.

I will try and explain the basics of the book and hopefully this will be helpful. However, reading *The Chimp Paradox* in full is advised for a clearer insight.

In simple terms, the brain is divided into three areas that Dr Peters describes as the Computer, the Human and the Chimp, which are all very different.

Starting with the Computer, this is the part of the brain that is full of experiences and memories built up throughout your whole life, and will include both good and bad experiences. Nearly every thought and subsequent action will be based in some way on your past experiences and therefore it is important to understand the significance of those experiences and that you can change how they affect you in a positive way. If you have had bad experiences in your life then the likelihood is that they will continue to have a detrimental effect on you long after the actual experience. You may not be aware of or realise the damaging effect they can have, but these 'gremlins' are likely always to be there unless you can address them by recognising them, understanding them, and then getting rid of them!

Example of a gremlin

Imagine being a ten-year-old at school, when the teacher asked a question of his pupils; you put your hand up and answered in front of the class. However, you misheard the question and your answer was very wrong. But worse than the fact that you had simply given a wrong answer, was that the rest of the children started laughing out loud, and even the teacher laughed at you. You felt incredibly embarrassed and upset and that feeling haunted you for ages. Ever since, you have become reluctant to speak out, answer questions, put your view across, for fear of this embarrassment happening again. You continue throughout your life being very wary and reluctant to speak up and your confidence is affected as a result.

Now let's look at this rationally and see if we can get rid of this gremlin. Firstly, we all make mistakes and get things wrong. Secondly, you were only ten years old and the children who laughed were only ten years old – you would probably have done the same. Thirdly, you misheard the question, which wasn't your fault. Finally, it was just one incident when you were very young – you cannot let this affect you any more. Acknowledge it happened and then rationally dispose of this gremlin. That situation will not happen again, so speak up, answer questions and you will regain confidence in this area.

Hopefully you will also have had good experiences and these are likely to continue to play a positive role in your life. Of course, the more positive experiences the better and it is important to recognise these as well as recognising the negative gremlins. The positive experiences are referred to as 'Auto-Pilots' and the aim is to increase the number of these by generating new positive experiences and also changing some of the bad experiences into positive ones, which can be possible.

The Human part of the brain is the real you and when this is active and working well then we are rational, logical, calm and mature, and our thoughts and behaviours are based upon facts and our core values. This is how we would want to behave most of the time and how we would want other people to behave. The human part of the brain has developed over hundreds of thousands of years and distinguishes us from other animals. Humans need purpose and fulfilment in their lives.

The Chimp part of the brain is at the core; it is the original part of the brain that existed before the human part developed and grew through evolution. When this part of the brain is active our behaviour can be very 'un-human' and our behaviours and thoughts are very much how we might expect a chimp to be. They will be very emotive, reactionary and impulsive, the main instinct being survival, with the options of fight, flight or freeze. So in this mood with the chimp in control we could be aggressive, excitable, anxious, scared, naughty etc. We are not rational, we don't look at the facts, we are not logical, and we are not mature.

Example of chimp and human behaviour

Let's imagine that you are going to an important meeting that is taking place at 2pm, and it is normally a thirty-minute drive or less to get to the location of the meeting. You decide to leave at 1.15pm to give yourself plenty of extra time to get there for 2pm. However, on the way, there is some unexpected traffic, a combination of roadworks, temporary traffic lights and a broken-down car. You start to feel agitated and annoyed, especially as nobody seems to be doing any actual roadworks and you expect it was the person's fault who broke down, causing the additional delay. You have given yourself some extra time, though, so you should still make the meeting on time. Once you are clear of the roadworks and traffic lights you then get stuck behind a really slow car and are not able to overtake. Your frustration builds and you become angrier and even more annoyed. You start to think you are going to be late for your important meeting.

Still stuck behind the slow car you decide to try a shortcut and drive through a housing estate, but quite soon, with lots of cars parked on the road, you have to stop to let an oncoming car go by. You stop and wait and let the car go by, but they do not wave to say thank you or acknowledge you in any way and you are outraged. You get so angry that you are fit to explode. You can no longer concentrate on the meeting because you are so worked up that you are late and people are so rude, and you finally arrive still angry, upset and agitated.

It is clear that you have been in chimp-behaviour mode! As a result of events, and other people's actions out of your control, you have let your chimp take over and make matters worse for you. You are upset and angry, and potentially the important meeting is compromised as a result. Now, if you were able to manage the chimp and have the human remain in control you would be in a much better position.

You would rationalise that you did allow plenty of extra time to get to the meeting and what happened was out of your control and you are not to blame. You would rationalise that there are always 'idiot' or 'rude' drivers out there but you cannot do anything about that. You would rationalise that the best thing for you would be to stay calm, not get upset, let it go, reassure yourself that it's not the end of the world, and gain some perspective on the situation. You would apologise for being a few minutes late and explain the new traffic lights and roadworks and remain in the right mood and frame of mind for the important meeting.

The human remains rational, calm and logical, whilst the chimp gets agitated, angry, upset, emotional and reactive. In this situation it is clear that it is better for you for the human to be in control and the chimp to be managed.

The important initial step is to recognise when you are thinking and behaving in chimp mode. If you ask yourself the question or reflect on the situation it will be fairly obvious whether you are in human or chimp mode. If you then recognise you are indeed in the latter then you have to work out how best to manage this and how the human can regain control. If the chimp's behaviour and thinking is around anger and aggression then it may be best to allow the chimp to have a short outburst but then quickly put him away in a cage to calm down. If the behaviour and thinking are more about being worried, anxious and scared then it may be best to reassure your chimp, give him or her a hug, providing protection and security.

Here is a simple chart explaining some of the key differences between the Human and the Chimp:

	HUMAN	CHIMP
Behaviours	Logical Rational Level-headed Mature Gets the Facts	Reactive Irrational Emotional Excitable Anxious Aggressive
Life is all about...	Purpose Fulfilment	Survival

Number 1 rule – Life is not fair

Unfortunately, it is true to say that life is unfair. So often things happen to us and other people, both directly and indirectly, that are not fair. It is not nice and it is not right but it is fact! The sooner you accept that life is not fair the better. Often in life, when negative things happen, there is nothing to blame or it is nobody's fault, it just happens and we have to move on and get on with improving our lives and doing what we can do.

Inner troop is very important

Your inner troop refers to those people that are closest to you and who you can trust, feel supported by, can depend on, and where there is a mutual respect. Those people who are positive for your life, help you to be a better person, lift you up when needed and are honest and truthful with you. Now you may expect that from all your family and friends, however this is rarely the case and too often you will find there are people in your life that do not fit the above description. These people have a negative effect on you and your life and wherever possible you need to get rid of them!

It is far better to have quality than quantity with your inner troop and it is important you make a real effort with these people to maintain and enhance the relationships of the troop. Drop those that are not good for you and have a negative and damaging impact on your life if you can. Your inner troop is very important to your happiness and confidence.

You can only do your best!

A further important message from The Chimp Paradox book that also impacts on confidence is the fact that you can only ever do your best. You cannot do better than your best – that's not possible! So whatever the situation or circumstance, if you have done your best, you should be happy, as you couldn't possibly have done any more. So no matter what the result or outcome is, be positive and proud that you have done your best. By doing your best, that is fantastic and a wonderful achievement and that should give you more confidence.

Identifying and managing the Chimp!

Practise identifying your chimp and human behaviour, and also other people's. Every day you will find yourself both in Chimp mode and in Human mode – when you make a concerted effort to recognise your behaviour, it is usually very clear what mode you are in!

When you find yourself in Chimp mode try to understand why. Ask yourself these questions:

- **What events, actions, people, circumstances etc. have made you act, think and behave in Chimp mode?**
- **Has being in Chimp mode helped you?**
- **Has it made things better for you?**
- **Do you regret anything you did or said whilst in Chimp mode?**

Developing techniques to manage the Chimp and allow the Human to take over:

Step 1 – First you have to recognise you are in Chimp mode.
Step 2 – Remind yourself that in most cases being in Chimp mode will not be beneficial for you.
Step 3 – Try to take a step back or a deep breath and think what a mature adult human would most likely do in that situation.
Step 4 – Think how best to manage the chimp in that particular situation. For example, does it need reassurance? Does it need to let off steam? Does it need to be put in a cage?
Step 5 – Remind yourself again that you are the human and can manage the situation and take control of the chimp.

Get out of your comfort zone

'Strength doesn't come from what you can do, it comes from overcoming the things you once thought you couldn't.' **– Rikki Rogers**

It is all too easy to live your life in your comfort zone and in many ways being 'comfortable' is a good thing. However, if you always remain in your comfort zone then you are missing out on so much and you are limiting what you could do, what you could achieve and the opportunity to live a much more fulfilling and happy life. Yes, there are some risks involved in 'getting out of your comfort zone' but the rewards on offer hugely outweigh those risks.

How many times during your life have you denied yourself the opportunity of doing something because it was out of your comfort zone? You were perhaps unsure, nervous, worried about what might happen, didn't believe you could do it, thought you wouldn't like it etc... and focused on the negatives and what might go wrong rather than thinking positively about what could happen.

I am also sure there have been times when you have stepped out of your comfort zone and been so glad you did. How many times have you, or other people you know, tried something and been so happy that you did. It won't always be the case, but I am a strong believer that probably, on average, eight times out of ten, you will be glad you did step out of your comfort zone... and they are great odds to take when you next find yourself deliberating whether you should or should not do something.

By getting out of your comfort zone and trying new things, you develop as a person, you gain new skills, learn new lessons, meet new people, open your eyes more, find out more about yourself, understand what you can do and it all helps build confidence. And this increased confidence means you will try new things even more and thus continue to grow, learn, improve and live your life more fully.

'A ship is safe in the harbour, but that's not what ships are for.'
– John A. Shedd
***'You can never cross the ocean unless you have the courage to lose sight of the shore.'* – Christopher Columbus**

There will be times when things don't go so well and you fail or the outcome is disappointing. You may be tempted to regret what you did, but rather than regret what you did, take it as another learning experience. Life is full of experiences, both good and bad, but when they are bad then you can still take the positives out of it, even if that is simply, don't try that again! Though more likely you will have learnt some really valuable lessons and increased your knowledge, which will help you in other situations.

'Take risks: if you win, you will be happy; if you lose, you will be wise.'

Finally in this section, we have to acknowledge that we all fail during our lives. Failure is inevitable and nobody has ever gone through their life without failing. Often the people who fail the most also achieve the most because from their failures they learn, pick themselves up and try again. They are more willing to try more, do more and thus achieve more. Nobody likes to fail, but the difference in attitude to failure is everything.

If you fail and let it define you in a negative way then you have a problem. It can ruin your confidence, play on your mind, stop you doing other things, make you feel depressed and you won't want to put yourself in a position again where failure could happen. However, if you embrace it by learning from the failure, understanding what happened and what you could do differently or what additional help or skills you need then that failure can be so good for you. By dealing with failures in a positive way, you can increase your confidence, your resilience, your skill set etc., and when you come again your chance of success will be much higher. So as the saying below says, when you fall you have two choices – stay on the floor or get up and go again.

'Our greatest glory is not in never falling, but in rising every time we fall.'

Confucius

Inspiring stories of successful failures!

Here are just a few examples of very successful people who have failed and been rejected, often many times. They have understood that not only is failure inevitable, it can be used in a positive and productive way. It helps shape the person you become and can provide the additional motivation and drive as well as knowledge to then succeed.

'Sometimes it is worth losing a battle to win the war.'

Michael Jordan

Undoubtedly the most famous and possibly the greatest basketball player of all time suffered failure and rejection and used that experience to help make him succeed. He was cut from the varsity basketball team in his sophomore year (second year) at college. At the time he simply wasn't good enough. He went home, closed the door to his room and cried his eyes out.

That single rejection became the launch pad for his basketball career. It gave him the motivation to dig deeper, train harder, play with greater intensity and quite simply he wanted it more.

Since his incredible career finished he has done a lot of work in the motivational field and a common quote from Michael Jordan that demonstrates his attitude towards failure is this:

'I've missed more than 9000 shots in my career. I've lost almost 300 games. 26 times, I've been trusted to take the game-winning shot and missed. I've failed over and over and over again in my life. And that is why I succeed.'

Walt Disney

One of the most famous names in the last one hundred years and known all around the world for his Disney characters, films, animations and theme parks, Walt Disney suffered many setbacks and rejections. He was fired from his job by his news editor because he lacked imagination, his first animation company went bankrupt and it took hundreds of rejections for finance before he finally raised the money needed for Disney World.

His drive, belief and confidence kept him going despite these failures and rejections and in many ways these adverse situations provided him with greater strength and motivation to succeed. A great quote from him is:

'All our dreams can come true if we have the courage to pursue them.'

J. K. Rowling

When J. K. Rowling wrote the first Harry Potter book she was penniless, recently divorced, raising a child on her own and depressed, and her manuscript was rejected twelve times over the course of a year before she finally got a publishing deal. She was rejected over and over again but she persevered to become one of the richest and best-known authors in the world.

When addressing a large group of students at Harvard University a few years ago she said:

'You might never fail on the scale I did, but it is impossible to live without failing at something, unless you live so cautiously that you might as well not have lived at all – in which case, you fail by default.'

Brian Acton

You may not be so familiar with Brian Acton but he is the multi-billionaire co-founder of WhatsApp. He was a software engineer for many years with varying success at Adobe, Apple and Yahoo, plus he invested and lost a lot of money in the first dot.com boom in the early 2000s. In 2009 he applied for jobs at both Facebook and Twitter but was rejected, so instead set up his own app with a former colleague he worked with at Yahoo – Jan Koum – and they called it WhatsApp. The rest is history and ironically, he later sold the business to Facebook.

Imagine what would, or rather what would not have happened, if he had got the job he applied for at both Facebook and Twitter. Rejection and disappointment can be a blessing in disguise. It can lead to other opportunities, make you more determined or try other things you wouldn't otherwise do.

Practical tips and advice to boost confidence

LISTEN TO YOUR OWN ADVICE

If a close friend told you they were lacking confidence, or were worried about certain issues, or a particular situation, what would be your advice to them? How would you help them boost their confidence or face up to the issue and overcome it? What factors would you consider and how would you advise them in the best way?

Now consider that the close friend needing the help is actually you. Listen to your own advice and act upon it. It is very likely that you will offer great advice that will definitely help.

'Nobody can give you wiser advice than yourself.' **- Cicero**

AVOID PERFECTIONISM

Many people have unrealistic expectations of themselves, and when these are not met they beat themselves up about it, which causes a mix of problems. Nobody is perfect and nobody can be perfect. There is nothing wrong with trying your best. In fact, trying your best is fantastic and should be encouraged, but there is usually a big difference between what someone sees as perfect and what is achievable when doing your best.

Your confidence will be damaged, you will be unhappy and disappointed, and you will cause yourself stress if you always expect perfection in what you do. Endeavour to do your best but recognise this is not about being perfect. Stop beating yourself up and being super-critical if you are not perfect.

STOP TRYING TO PLEASE EVERYONE

A common problem we have is trying to please other people all the time, and often we find the more we lack confidence, the more we focus on trying to please others rather than focusing on ourselves. You can never please everyone. So you will always fail if you try to do this. It is your life and you are the most important person to try and please, and when you feel good you will automatically benefit those people in your life that you care about. Be kind to yourself.

Worry less about what others think, stop trying to seek approval or recognition from people, live your life according to your values and focus on what is best for you rather than trying to please everyone else all the time. It will take effort and practice but you can do this.

DON'T AVOID

If you find yourself avoiding things, people and situations and have become more withdrawn and reclusive, you need to work on this to make sure it doesn't get worse. Sometimes it is advisable and beneficial to avoid certain situations, but the danger is that you can soon end up losing important social skills and becoming more distant from people and places, restricting your opportunities to enjoy life and have more positive experiences.

Build up slowly if you have found yourself in this position. At first you may look to get outside your house and go for a walk on your own for a short while. Next time you may make the effort to say 'hello' to someone you pass on your walk. You may then go to a busier area like a shopping centre where there are many people about but you don't have to engage with them. The next step may be to have a short conversation with a cashier or assistant at a shop by asking them a question or wishing them a pleasant day. Gradually you are building up your contact with other people step by step and gaining confidence in those situations. You may try to meet up with a friend for a coffee and chat and look to make more conversations with people, whether that's at work, at the shops or with other friends. Over time you will develop improved social skills and confidence so that you are more comfortable and at ease in those situations.

FINGER/THUMB

If you are in a situation where you feel you need an instant boost of confidence – for example, about to do a presentation, go for a job interview, go on a first date, about to start a race, or halfway through an exam – then this technique can be quite effective. Firstly, think about someone you admire and respect, perhaps a hero or mentor. It could be someone you know personally or someone you haven't met but is a huge inspiration to you. Think about this person and all the positives and reasons why you have chosen them.

Then if you are ever in need of a confidence boost, rather than crossing your fingers and just hoping, you can squeeze your finger and thumb together and think about this person. Think about their qualities, why they are an inspiration, and what they would do in this situation. Let their inspiration boost your confidence. Try it!

FIVE REGRETS ON YOUR DEATHBED

I don't know if this is actually true, but in a way it doesn't matter because the sentiment and message is very clear. A survey was carried out in Australia by a nurse at a hospital treating terminally ill patients, and the top five regrets of those people who were dying were as follows:

I wish I'd had the courage to live a life true to myself, not the life others expected of me.
I wish I hadn't worked so hard.
I wish I'd had the courage to express my feelings.
I wish I'd stayed in touch with my friends.
I wish that I had let myself be happier.

Take some time to think about this. What can you visualise yourself saying if you were in that same position? Be honest and reflective and write down your own list. What does that tell you?

Remember, you only get one life but you get lots of opportunities. Make the most of those opportunities.

POSITIVE PAST MEMORIES

It is very likely that you have some positive memories from the past that can provide a confidence boost to you. Think about situations, events or experiences that you have had that have been really positive on a personal level. Recall the feeling, the pride, the passion, the success, the achievement, and use it to inspire, motivate and boost your confidence in the present moment.

For example, I have completed several marathons and on each one I can remember crossing the finishing line with the crowds cheering and the mix of positive emotions, the feeling of relief yet elation, the personal achievement and pride making the pain and sacrifice worth it, and the confidence gained from doing that and thinking *If I can do this then I can do anything*! If I need a confidence boost, or some extra motivation while training then I have a bank of these experiences that I can use to help. Create your own bank of positive memories and call upon them when you need to.

FIND A MENTOR

If you are lucky enough to have a good mentor in your life then you will know how beneficial they can be. A good mentor is a person you can talk to, seek advice from, discuss issues with and whom you trust and who has your best interests at heart; someone who has experience, knowledge and wisdom that can be passed on to you in order to help you develop as a person, which in turn adds to your confidence.

If you don't have a mentor, then why not see if you can find one. Make some effort to identify a person you respect and trust who can offer some of their time and experiences that will be beneficial for you. Perhaps it could be someone at work, possibly a family member or friend of a friend. If you believe they could be a good mentor then ask them if they would consider filling that role. It may not work out, but if you don't try you won't know, and if it does work then the added value and benefits will be worth it.

MUSIC

Listening to your favourite music, especially upbeat and positive tracks, can really lift your mood. It can release some adrenaline, increase your energy and boost your confidence. Whether it's before you go out, ahead of a meeting, in the build-up to a race or challenge, prior to a presentation you are delivering, or just for more general situations, it is definitely worth trying.

Music is usually readily available at home, in the car, on your computer, or phone etc., so take advantage and try it. Play music that you associate with happy memories – a holiday, a party, an event when you were relaxed and confident, enjoying your life heartily. And as long as it is appropriate then why not try singing aloud or dancing around to the music too!

WEAR A SCENT

If you don't already then wear a scent – perfume, aftershave, eau de toilette etc. – take a bit of time to find the one you like and use it. Research has shown that this can increase confidence as it makes you feel better and more secure as well as smelling nice of course, plus you are likely to get more compliments as a result.

ACT LIKE A CONFIDENT PERSON

Many people who appear confident are in fact acting. They are able to put on a front when needed and act like a confident person. With a little bit of practice you can also do this and your confidence is likely to improve as a result of acting like a confident person.

Imagine how you would think, act and behave if you were a confident person and then look to replicate that for real and become an actor. You may find it easier to act in this way in an environment away from your normal situation. So perhaps if you go away for a weekend, or visit a new town or shopping centre, or when you meet a new group of people, then this can be your opportunity to practise acting like a confident person. It may feel strange but there is a good chance that you can pull it off and you feel more comfortable acting this way, and it becomes more normal the more you practise. Going forward you may also find the gap between *acting* like a confident person and actually *being* a confident person becomes smaller and smaller.

HANDLE CRITICISM

It is likely that there will be times throughout your life when you will be criticised for something. On occasions this will be justified and on others it will be unfair and unjustified. However, your ability to handle criticism is very important. If it is justified then the ability to take on board the criticism and look to make positive changes to improve is necessary. Do not become defensive and closed to constructive feedback and criticism. Understand, accept and then look to improve. Too often people become very defensive and take criticism very badly, and when it is justified it means they will continue making the same mistakes.

Also, it is important to be able to handle criticism when it is unfair and not justified – being able to ignore it, forget it, let it go and move on without it affecting you adversely. This can be difficult, but unless you develop tools and techniques to ignore the unfair and unjust criticism it can eat away at you and cause problems, especially regarding your confidence. Everyone has a right to an opinion but that doesn't mean it is right. Often the unfair criticism will not be based on facts or take into account all the factors, or the critic's knowledge will be limited or they have their own personal issues going on that distort their view. So take this into account and if you feel this is the case then let it go and move on.

LEARN TO SAY NO

For many people it is very difficult to say no to other people and often as a result they get taken advantage of, which is not in their best interests and usually decreases their confidence further. They become a soft touch and end up doing things they don't want to do and become frustrated and upset as a result. They can't seem to end the cycle, as the more they say yes the more it happens and the lower their confidence becomes.

The ability to say no can be really important. Being able to stand up for yourself, being more assertive and saying no when you believe that saying no is the right thing to do, are characteristics of a confident person. So if you are lacking confidence it is harder to do and compounds the problem. But once you learn to say no it becomes easier. You gain confidence and feel more comfortable in standing up for yourself and being more assertive. Try it, practise it and you will feel much better as a result.

NERVOUS FACE

Here is a quick exercise that can be fun and also very effective in combating nerves. Stand in front of a mirror and pull a 'happy/smiley/joyful' face. Next pull a 'sad/upset/miserable' face. Next pull a 'shocked/surprised' face. Finally, pull a 'nervous' face.

What did you notice? Hopefully you will realise that it is usually very obvious what the emotion is, whether that's happy, sad or shocked, due to the facial expressions that the person shows. But when it comes to being nervous there is literally no emotion. It is a blank, still, emotionless expression that comes across. There is nothing that shows or expresses your nerves and anxiety.

So when you are in that situation where you are nervous and anxious and you are worried that everyone will know how nervous you are then just remember they cannot tell from your facial expression. There is no expression of nerves, therefore they will not know, and you can be reassured that people won't be thinking how nervous you are.

PEOPLE

As previously discussed, the people around you can have a big impact on your confidence both positively and negatively. So if you have people you know that impact on you positively then try to meet them, spend time with them, talk to them and let their qualities help you to increase your confidence. They will want to help and you may decide to tell them the positive effect they have. What a great compliment to receive from someone! You may need to make an effort, take a bit of extra time out or travel to see them but it will be worth it in order to feel better and get that confidence boost.

Also, you can ask friends what they most like about you and what they think your best qualities are. You can let them know that you are feeling a bit low in confidence and the responses they give will almost certainly remind you of some of your great qualities. Listen to the compliments, accept them, and most importantly, never ignore them, and use them to have a more positive and confident outlook.

'Confidence is contagious. So is lack of confidence.'
Vince Lombardi

VISUALISE

A well-known and often effective technique that can be used is to visualise what you want actually happening. The more you visualise it the more likely it is to happen. With visualisation usually comes focus and if it is a positive focus you are also more likely to believe it will happen and be more confident the outcome will be the one you want.

It could be visualising a job interview going well, so rather than worrying about saying something wrong or not coming across well, you are instead visualising a great interview, focusing on the positives. It could be during a running race you are finding things tough but you start to visualise yourself crossing the finish line, succeeding in your goals, feeling the sense of achievement and pride and how positive that is. It could be attending a new group event and visualising lots of nice, friendly, welcoming people and feeling comfortable and enjoying the occasion.

By visualising particular situations in a positive way with positive outcomes you are being productive and it will help give you the confidence to go ahead with that situation rather than worrying about it.

MAKEOVER

Take some time to give yourself a treat of a makeover. Perhaps it could be a new haircut or style, buy some new clothes, go for a facial or other beauty treatment or you could buy a new perfume or aftershave to wear. Make some effort and invest some time and money (appropriately) for yourself.

If you take that time and make that investment you will feel better about how you look and feel as well as how you come across to others, which will naturally boost your confidence. Other people are also likely to notice and you may get some additional compliments and positive feedback as a bonus, although what *you* think and how *you* feel is the most important thing.

JOKES, FACTS, STORIES

You will all know people who always seem to have something interesting to say, stories to tell, facts they can recall and jokes they share. They generally come across as interesting, funny, intelligent and confident. Wouldn't it be good to have these skills and be able to do similarly if the opportunity arises? How great would it feel if you could do this and people thought you were all those things? You would undoubtedly feel more confident.

Well, there is no reason why you can't improve on this by learning some jokes, reading more books, learning more facts, watching more news and current affairs, thinking about some great stories and examples from your own life. It may help to write them down, think about them more, practise telling them etc., so that if and when the opportunity arises, you feel more comfortable sharing these stories, facts and jokes. Step by step you will feel more confident and comfortable in group conversations and by participating you won't feel left out, you won't be sitting there wishing you could join in and feeling negative about that. With some effort you can really build your confidence in this way.

LEARN TO LAUGH AT YOURSELF

Do you take yourself too seriously? When you do something wrong or stupid or make a mistake do you beat yourself up about it? Are you particularly hard on yourself, not giving yourself a break especially when things don't go as you would like them to? Do you ever smile and laugh at yourself when you do sometimes make a mistake?

We all make mistakes; we all do stupid things at times or get things wrong. Sometimes it is best just to laugh at yourself. Understand that you are not perfect and it is OK to do something stupid occasionally. When something goes wrong try laughing at the situation rather than beating yourself up and getting upset or angry. It won't always work but at times the best thing to do is just laugh at yourself and not take things quite so seriously. Your confidence will be dented if you always blame yourself, get upset, beat yourself up, or get angry at mistakes you make. So practise smiling and laughing at yourself more and it might just be a good thing.

'If at first you don't succeed, try, try again. Then quit. There's no use being a damn fool about it.'

W.C. Fields

NEW SKILLS

Are you impressed if someone has a skill or a natural aptitude for something? Do you have more respect for them? Do you see them in a more positive light? There are so many skills that you could learn that will help build confidence. Examples could include learning a foreign language, painting, photography, writing, juggling, martial arts, cooking, and the list could go on and on. It could be a new skill that is relevant to your career or simply a new hobby. But learning a new skill will have many benefits and is very likely to help increase your confidence, so think about things you may wish to do and look at how you could go about learning these new skills.

By learning a new skill, the chances are that you may have contact with others who have the same goals and this will enable you to interact with like-minded people. Immediately you have met others on common ground and this will enable you to be more relaxed and confident.

MOTIVATION

Why is motivation so important?

You will all know from personal experience that if you are motivated to do something then you are far more likely to do it, to get it done quicker, to succeed, to achieve and enjoy whatever it is. Being motivated to do something means you will be more focused, determined, inspired and resilient. All of these things are positive and make you more productive, which means you are more likely to be fulfilling a particular purpose that we know is fundamental to your happiness, and the achievement and feelings you get from this have such a positive impact on your life.

So it stands that if you are able to be more motivated more of the time then you will be much happier in life. But we all know it can be hard to be motivated! However, by understanding what motivation is, the huge rewards you can get from increased motivation and practical ways to achieve this, then you are far more likely to improve things.

How often do we procrastinate, put things off, not try, not commit to something, talk ourselves out of something, say we will do it tomorrow, next week or next year? Or we give up, turn back, stop trying, take the easier option or convince ourselves we will do it again at a later date. When this happens then we don't get the results and outcomes we want, plus there is often a sense of failure or even shame. It is not a good feeling and undoubtedly lowers our confidence. So what can we do about it? Well hopefully, this section will help by understanding more about motivation and then providing practical tips and advice to increase our motivation that will then lead to doing more, achieving more, increasing confidence and this, in turn, creates even more motivation.

'Understanding motivation is one of the most important things we can do in our lives, because it has such a bearing on why we do the things we do and whether we enjoy them or not.'
Clayton Christensen

What is motivation?

The formal dictionary definition of 'motivation' is '**a *reason or reasons for acting or behaving in a particular way***'.

The psychological definition of 'motivation' is ***'the process that initiates, guides and maintains goal-orientated behaviours. It involves the biological, emotional, social and cognitive forces that activate behaviour.'***

I have also asked a number of people for their own definition of motivation; here is a selection of the responses:

- Motivation is an inner feeling that produces the incentive to undertake an activity or action. It is usually a strong feeling that provokes a reaction into doing/completing something that you might not otherwise do.
- Motivation is having the desire to take action, do something and whether it is something you are happy or even excited about doing.
- Motivation is the desire and 'will' to do something and get things done. To achieve a goal, no matter how small.
- Motivation is having the willpower and energy to do something positive. It is what causes us to act on the goals we want to achieve and to get the end results.
- Motivation is something that provides somebody with the inclination to do something.
- Motivation is having a purpose to achieve and achieve well. It is gaining respect from others and self-worth for yourself. It's a reason

to get up in the morning.
- Motivation is the will and confidence to complete any task and encompassing the reasons for doing something.

I believe there are four key components of motivation, as follows:
The starting point – there has to be an initial starting point for your motivation, perhaps a goal or challenge you have thought of, or someone else has planted an idea that sparks an interest. From this initial point there comes the activation of the idea and you start to plan and prepare until you actually commit to that particular goal. The motivation is usually quite high in the initial stages with a burst of optimism and enthusiasm.
Endurance – this is how long you can maintain the effort, and your level of persistence. It will require endurance and stamina to keep motivated so that you can achieve the goal. Are you able to keep going, overcome any hurdles or setbacks and persist with your efforts?
Intensity of effort – then there is how committed you really are to the goal, how much effort and hard work you will dedicate to the challenge and how much you want it. Are you prepared to give it your best, to focus, to make sacrifices and to keep motivating yourself so that the goal is achieved?
The end goal – finally there is the reward and sense of achievement you get from completing the goal and challenge. By focusing on the end result and reminding yourself of the reasons for the challenge and the benefits of achieving your goals you will be better placed to maintain your motivation.
All four components are important in order to be successful. If any one of them is missing or neglected then you are more likely to struggle with your motivation and therefore less likely to achieve your goals.

What do you want to be motivated for?

You have sought this book for a reason – so there must be things you want to do and achieve or be more motivated to do. Perhaps it is to achieve a physical challenge or maybe to lose weight and get fitter. Or it could be to be more effective and achieve more at work or you just want to get more out of life and do more things. Spend a few minutes thinking about what you want to achieve, why you want to be motivated and what challenges and goals you want to set for yourself.

Write these thoughts down here:

What stops you being motivated?

There are many possible factors that contribute towards a lack of motivation or which can stop you being motivated altogether. Below are examples that people have given of factors that can stop you being motivated. Have a read through and be honest with yourself by identifying those that you can relate to. Once you become more aware of the factors that cause the motivational issues then the better position you will be in to address them and look at ways to overcome them. The examples given are not exhaustive, so you may think of others not mentioned, and many of them may not apply to you, but read through and make sure you are honest about those that do apply.

But before you do read on please take some time to list your own examples of what stops you being motivated! Use the box below to identify and then write down all those factors, reasons and excuses that affect your motivation:

Depression

There are many symptoms of depression and many of these will make it difficult to become motivated. You are likely to have a lot of negative thoughts and behaviours, your confidence and self-esteem is likely to be low, you will often feel tired and lack energy, you may have problems sleeping, you may turn to comfort eating or not eat enough, drug and alcohol issues may occur and your general appetite for life will be reduced. So, there are many potential symptoms that will make it more difficult to get motivated, yet the depression will be helped significantly if you are able to do many of the things that require motivation. There is a catch-22 scenario here, so it is therefore even more important to understand more about depression and motivation in order that both can be improved.

Tiredness/lack of energy

Your motivation will often be limited when you feel tired, lethargic and lacking energy. It is so much more difficult to find the will and motivation to do things when feeling tired or exhausted. So it is important to try and work out the reasons and causes for feeling tired. Is it stress, lack of sleep, poor diet, too much alcohol, not enough exercise, worry, anxiety, illness, trying to do too much, or a combination of any of these? There will always be an explanation, so you need to try and find out those causes and look to address them, otherwise you will continue to struggle with motivation.

Negative people

There will always be people in your life who are negative and not very supportive. This could be for a variety of reasons and they could be people at work, family members or even your friends. They may say things that demotivate you, making you feel that your goals are not worth it or not achievable. They may point out all the risks, dangers and downsides rather than looking at all the positives. It could be due to jealousy, their own personal issues or other factors, but whatever the reason, they are causing you problems if their negativity impacts on your motivation to achieve things, move forward and become happier. If possible you have to try and remove these negative people from your life or at least learn to ignore them.

'You cannot hang out with negative people and expect to live a positive life.' **Joel Osteen**

Anxiety

Many people suffer with anxiety to a greater or lesser extent, including some who have panic attacks. Feeling some nerves and being a little apprehensive is normal, expected and can be advantageous in many situations but if your anxiety is more than this and actually prevents you from doing things then this is a problem that needs to be addressed. Try to understand the reasons behind the anxiety and seek appropriate help. This could be medication, counselling, meditation, CBT (Cognitive Behavioural Therapy), talking to friends, relaxation techniques etc. Anxiety can be managed and overcome, but you need to work at it and then you will be able to do and achieve so many more things, and the worry will be replaced by increased motivation.

Not feeling appreciated

It is always nice to be appreciated, especially if you have put lots of effort into something, so if you don't feel appreciated or expect an outcome to be unappreciated then it is likely to decrease your motivation. You may think, what is the point if nobody cares and nobody appreciates what I am doing? Of course, it is important to get recognition in some way for your efforts and feel appreciated, but it is even more important that you can appreciate yourself and be proud of what you have achieved. Do not let others' behaviour stop you doing what is right and beneficial for you.

Stress

A little bit of stress is usually a good thing in that it can help you focus and concentrate and be more efficient in your delivery; however, too much stress can have very negative consequences. Many people will become so stressed that they are unable to perform well, to concentrate, to think clearly and to achieve things as they would wish. It can become increasingly difficult to motivate yourself the more stressed you feel, and stress can cause a lack of energy too and drain you of energy. So, think carefully about your stress levels and how you can reduce and manage them so they do not impact upon your motivation.

Worrying about outcome

If more of your time, effort and thinking is worrying about the outcome and whether you will be successful or not then this is likely to have an adverse effect on your motivation to achieve your goal. Worrying is a negative and unproductive emotion and behaviour and will make you question yourself and whether your goal is worth pursuing. If you plan, prepare and commit to something and give it your best effort then that is all you can do. If, instead, you are worrying about what will happen you are far more likely to give up and not succeed and your motivation will decrease further.

Thinking about past issues

You may find yourself thinking about past experiences that could include issues you've faced or failures that have happened and, therefore, you will again be focusing more on the negatives than on the positives. This is likely to reduce your motivation, and your attention will be more on these factors than on the actual goal or challenge you currently want to achieve. You can learn from the past and use this to your benefit, but just because something hasn't worked out previously does not mean that will happen again.

Fear of failing

One of the biggest fears people have is the fear of failure and this is very relevant with regard to motivation. If you fear that the outcome will result in failure then you are more likely to give up and not succeed. You will be less motivated because of the fear, whereas if you did not fear failing then you would be much more positive, enthusiastic, determined and motivated. We all fail and it could happen, but there are no benefits to fearing failure. If you do fail for whatever reasons then you will be able to deal with those, yet if you are not motivated because of a fear of failure then you will not give yourself the best chance to be successful. Remember that even the top athletes come second or even lower placed in some races, yet they are 100% committed to winning.

Not believing in yourself

If you lack self-belief it will be much harder to motivate yourself and achieve things. Firstly you will limit your challenges both in volume and difficulty, and secondly you are less likely to be able to motivate yourself and much more likely to give up. Believing you can do something then proving it, is a great source of motivation, so it is important you believe you can do something, no matter how small, and each time you do achieve your self-belief will increase, making it easier the next time.

Lack of confidence

In a similar way to having a lack of self-belief, if you have low confidence then you are likely to dwell on the negatives of a challenge and think that you will not succeed. Any slight setbacks are much more likely to have a disproportionately negative effect and increase your chances of giving up or not making the required effort. Confidence can be gained through achievement, and motivation is often the key to achievement, so it is essential that you look at both aspects and build slowly and surely, because each time you achieve something both motivation and achievement will increase.

Loneliness

Many people gain motivation from friends, family and colleagues yet many others find themselves feeling very lonely and they do not have the support, contact and involvement of other people. This loneliness can be a factor, making it much harder to find motivation. It can be tougher trying to do things on your own or not having other people to motivate you or participate with you in your goals and challenges. If you can find the right people to get involved so you feel less isolated and lonely then you are more likely to improve your motivation and want to do those things you need to do in order to achieve your goals.

Lack of money

For some goals and challenges you wish to achieve, money, or rather a lack of money, can be a factor. This could be due to financial risk, cost of equipment or materials, personal debt or other financial priorities. You need to make decisions on what it is worth to you, how much you are willing to invest, how to prioritise your money in the best way, or look at alternatives where money is less of an issue. There are so many goals and achievements that require little or no money or for which you can find a way of gaining the required money, that there is no need to give up or lack motivation purely because of lack of money.

Weather

It is quite common for people to cite the weather as a reason for not doing something or for their motivation to be affected as a result of the weather being too cold, too hot, too wet, too windy, too gloomy etc. However, in most cases it is rare that the weather actually prevents you doing something or achieving your goals. It is more about maintaining your motivation if the weather is unfavourable by having the right attitude, the right clothing and equipment and taking any necessary precautions to ensure appropriate safety. Make sure you are not someone who uses the weather as an excuse!

No passion, or lack of interest

It is definitely the case that if you are more passionate about something and have a real interest in it then you will find it easier to be more motivated. If what you are trying to achieve does not interest you much or you lack passion or excitement about the goal then it can be a problem. Is it possible to get passionate about it? Do you really need to do it or is it perhaps something you don't need to do? Or can you focus on all the benefits of achieving the goal and still get motivated for it even though you lack the genuine desire and passion?

Lack of time

Not having enough time is a very common reason for not doing something and being motivated, and conversely not being motivated enough means it is much more difficult to find the time to do something. Too often, though, using a lack of time is just an excuse and if you really want to do something then you will find the time. You need to look to improve your time management, set priorities and focus on the benefits of your goals so that it spurs you on to make the necessary time.

Children and family

If you have a family then it is likely they are your priority, whether that's your children, partner, parents etc. You may find yourself limited in what you can do because so much time, effort and focus is on them and it can become difficult to motivate yourself to achieve your own goals. But if you can be motivated to achieve things then this is likely to bring rewards that will benefit not just yourself but your whole family. You can use your family and children as a reason to motivate yourself rather than as a reason not to be motivated and achieve your goals.

Fear of what others will think

If you are worried about what people think, or fear what they might think about your particular goals and challenges then it will become harder to motivate yourself. Too often you don't do what is best for you and what you want to achieve because of the fear of what others will think about it. That is a real shame and something that needs to be overcome, otherwise the same problem will always exist and prevent you from achieving things and being happier. Remember this saying:

'A lion doesn't concern himself with the opinion of a sheep.'
– George R. R. Martin

Job and career

For most people their job and career is important to them. It not only provides income to support them, but it may be needed to support their family, it also provides them with a purpose and it can offer fulfilment. However, sometimes it can take over our lives to the point where we don't make time for other things. Of course there can be many goals and challenges to achieve workwise, but if there are things you want to achieve outside work then it is important to do them without letting work become a reason for poor motivation.

'Never get so busy making a living that you forget to make a life.'

Burden of expectation

Modern society brings many benefits yet also many responsibilities, expectations and pressure. Also there are so many things you can be doing, decisions to make, people to please, and you can find yourself overloaded with what you should be doing with your time. What is the best thing to focus on, what is the best use of your time and what should you be doing in order to meet the expectations you, your work, your friends, your family or society in general places upon you? This burden of expectation can cause a lack of clarity in achieving goals that can then lead to a lowering of motivation.

Distractions or lack of focus

If you have particular goals or challenges you want to achieve and succeed in then you need to be careful not to lose your focus and become distracted. If you do get distracted then it might be due to low motivation, but any distractions in themselves are likely to lead to your being even less motivated because your goals will take longer, your performance won't be as good and your appetite for achievement on those goals will diminish. Keep reminding yourself of why you want to achieve the goals and prioritise those above the distractions that can occur in daily life so that you can remain focused.

Feeling you might be wasting your time

If you set yourself goals and put in the time and effort required to achieve them, but at the same time you are questioning whether you may be wasting your time, then you may find your motivation for completing those goals decreases. Nobody wants to waste their time and if you feel that might be the case then it will be much harder to find the motivation to carry on. Remind yourself why you want to achieve the goals and why success in them is important. If it is something you want to do and it will bring benefits, rewards and happiness then it certainly can't be a waste of time.

Scared

There may be particular goals or challenges that put you outside your comfort zone and you may feel vulnerable or scared. Inevitably being outside your comfort zone makes you feel uncomfortable and being scared is likely to have a negative effect on your motivation. You don't want to feel scared so you may stop trying to achieve the goal. However, if you focus on the benefits and the fact that it is good at times to push yourself out of your normal comfort zone then you can have a more positive attitude, and once you achieve your goal you will know that in the future you don't need to feel scared.

Injury

Particularly when it comes to physical goals and challenges it can be very demotivating if you get injured and this then hinders your progress or stops you achieving your desired goals. Obviously it depends on the type and severity of the injury, but too often it will cause your motivation to plunge and lead you to giving up. However, if you get the right advice, do the right rehabilitation, be patient, be sensible and reset the goals in an appropriate way then injuries don't have to stop you achieving your goals. Or you can look to reshape your goals taking into account your injury.

Illness

In a similar way to being injured, having an illness can be very difficult to deal with and will often lower your motivation to achieve particular goals. Depending on the illness it can set you back several days or weeks, it can make you feel tired, set your training back, lower your confidence or derail your plans altogether. However, most illnesses will pass fairly quickly and with no lasting damage, so, although you may have to alter your goals a little, you should still focus on them and not let a temporary issue stop you achieving the bigger-picture goals you want.

Setbacks

Unfortunately in life, no matter who you are, you will experience setbacks, and often when you are not expecting them. So you may find yourself losing motivation due to setbacks you encounter either directly related to your goals or in an unrelated way. The important thing is how you handle those setbacks and refuse to let them deter you from maintaining your motivation and achieving your goals. Focus back on your reasons for the challenges you've set and it may be possible for any setbacks to actually increase your desire, determination and motivation to succeed.

Relationships

You may find yourself losing motivation for goals you have set due to other priorities taking over, such as an existing or new relationship. You could find yourself being discouraged by your partner for a variety of reasons or you could be facing a break-up or relationship difficulties whereby your motivation for other goals and challenges is compromised. Relationships are very important; however, achieving goals is also important and will often improve relationships, so be careful if you find your motivation falling.

Lack of respect

Success can be perceived differently by different people and can come in many formats; often a key measure of success is about gaining the respect of others. If you find yourself working hard on your goals, yet there seems to be a lack of respect from others for what you are doing then this can be very demotivating. You may question what you are doing and why, and if you feel there is a lack of respect you may give up on your aims. However, if your goals are important to you then that should outweigh anything else and you can't let doubters and sceptics stop you from achieving success for yourself.

Habit

If you have often found yourself becoming demotivated whilst trying to attempt challenges and achieve goals for whatever reason then it is likely you will get into a habit of the same feelings, thoughts and behaviours. This will then make it easier to give up, feel down and lack the drive and the motivation to continue. Don't let that become a habit; instead make your habits positive and productive and the more you are able to keep motivated the easier and more habitual that becomes too.

Spiral of demotivation – domino effect

From the above examples of factors that can cause motivational issues it is clear there are many and it is not always easy to stay motivated. The more possible factors that influence your thinking and behaviour in a negative way, the more likely it is that you will become demotivated. This can lead to a domino or a downward-spiralling effect that makes it increasingly more difficult to stay motivated or to regain your motivation once it begins to fall away. It is really important to recognise at the earliest stages that you are losing your motivation so that you can try to address it as soon as possible. The further you let it go the harder it becomes. So we will now focus on the reasons why motivation is important to you and the various tips, tools and advice that will hopefully help keep you motivated and indeed help to increase your motivation.

At this point you should take time to reflect on what you have read in this section. Can you identify with any of these? How do they affect you? Prioritise two or three that you particularly want to focus on, moving forward.

Why do you want to be motivated?

So we have looked at a long list of factors that may stop us being motivated and therefore may prevent us from achieving things that will benefit us. These factors can become genuine reasons, but more likely they are excuses. Try to establish whether they are excuses, and if so you need to see them as excuses rather than reasons. Then you can more easily stop using them, and the benefit of being motivated and achieving goals will outweigh the negative and damaging excuses.

If there are genuine reasons still on your list it becomes a case of understanding the reasons more clearly and seeking to overcome them if possible. There shouldn't be many reasons if you have been really honest with yourself, but where they do still exist it is likely they will always be a factor unless you work on them and work out how you can move forward without them holding you back.

You wouldn't be reading this book if you didn't want to be motivated, so it is a fairly safe assumption that you want to be happier, more fulfilled and achieve certain things in your life. Motivation is vital in order to be successful in challenges, goals, targets and other forms of personal achievement. Without motivation it is too easy to give up, not put the required effort or time in, not plan or prepare sufficiently and limit your ambitions with goals you set yourself.

So we are going to now look at a range of tips and advice that should help improve your motivation and, as with most things, it is really important to firstly understand each area that could help and then apply it as best you can, and then keep practising it or using the advice in the most effective way in your particular circumstances.

***'If it is important to you, you will find a way. If not, you will find an excuse.'* – Ryan Blair**

How do you get motivated?

We have looked at the definition of motivation and why it is important in order to achieve goals and challenges, to be successful and as a result to be happier. We have also looked at some of the many factors that can impact negatively on your motivation levels. Now we will look at how you can get motivated, stay motivated or regain your motivation effectively.

This is not easy and will require effort, honesty, resilience and practice but the rewards and benefits of good motivation will always be worth it – and the more you achieve, the more motivated you can be, then the easier it will become. So read through the following section carefully and also think about other things you could do that may not be documented here. If you find yourself struggling at all, then keep coming back to them, reread the advice and keep practising. Don't be afraid to change things if needed or to seek different or new methods to keep your motivation high, and always look forward towards the goals and the reasons you want to achieve them.

'First I dream my painting. Then I paint my dream.'
Vincent van Gogh

Your health is most important

Most people, if they step back and reflect, will agree that their health is extremely important and far too often they will take it for granted. It is usually only once ill or injured or suffering with a health issue that people realise just how important their health is. It is, in fact, the most important thing. A significant number of health issues are self-inflicted as a result of our lifestyle and choices we make with our health.

So, a great way of being motivated is actually to recognise how important your health is and how you can make a huge difference to your health with the activities you choose to do. Both your physical and mental health can be greatly improved by being healthier – exercising, eating better, drinking less alcohol, not smoking or taking drugs, achieving goals, enjoying life more etc.

Rewards

There is usually some kind of tangible reward involved in achieving a goal or a particular challenge that can help keep you motivated. Probably the most obvious reward is a financial one. Money can be a big motivator for many people, so if money is a motivator for you then a financial reward will help your motivation. It could be a bonus payment at work or a chance for a promotion based on your efforts that keep you motivated. Alternatively, you may be able to incentivise yourself financially even if there is no direct monetary gain from elsewhere. For example, you may reward yourself with something like a holiday, a car, a new phone etc., if you successfully achieve a certain goal.

Feeling good by helping others

If your aims and goals have the additional effect of helping others then this will usually make you feel good too. There is a lovely feeling of satisfaction knowing that your efforts and work have benefited other people, whether they are close to you like friends and family or complete strangers. If you know that you are helping others then this is likely to spur you on more and help with your motivational levels.

'A candle loses nothing of its light by lighting another candle.'
James Keller

Enthusiastic/positive people

We have previously discussed how negative people can be a factor in lowering motivation, but conversely if you have positive and enthusiastic people around you and helping then this can be a huge advantage. Enthusiasm can become infectious and if the environment and atmosphere is a vibrant, positive and upbeat one then it inherently produces better results and helps to increase motivation for the challenges faced. So seek out those types of people who will add value, support you, energise you and motivate you, as their support and encouragement can make a big difference.

'Be the most enthusiastic person you know!'

Encouragement

If you are being encouraged and you feel supported then you are more likely to stay motivated and put in the required effort to achieve your goals. Encouragement can be very powerful as it shows people care and want you to succeed. If you can find people who will provide that encouragement, energy and inspiration then it will most likely make a big difference and you will want to stay focused, keep going and stay motivated. You may need to explain to some people your objectives and reasons so that they understand why it is important to you, and that will enable them to offer you more encouragement and support.

Friends and family

Friends and family can be very powerful in determining your motivation, both in a good way and a bad way. We have seen that some friends and family members can be very negative and damaging for a variety of reasons, but if you have good friends and family who genuinely care and support you then their involvement can produce great results. Having that love, that support, that encouragement, that assistance and that help can be very motivational.

Time and deadlines

A lack of time is often used as an excuse not to achieve things, yet you can actually use this to your benefit in increasing motivation. If you give yourself deadlines and time-specific goals then you are more likely to work efficiently and effectively towards achieving them. Managing your time is important, as is keeping focused, but you are likely to get more done if you do have a degree of time pressure on you so it really focuses you and reduces other distractions. So think about how you can set realistic but challenging deadlines and you are likely to improve motivation as a result.

Prove to yourself

Often a particular goal, aim or challenge is very personal to the individual undertaking it and it becomes very much about proving to yourself you can do it. This personal achievement and proving something important to yourself can be a very powerful motivating factor. If you can succeed in this goal and thus prove to yourself that you can do it then this can boost confidence, self-belief, self-respect and, of course, make you feel happy, boosting your endorphins and generally lifting your mood.

Respect

Another powerful result of achieving goals is the respect you create for yourself and gain from other people. Knowing that your efforts have been rewarded in some way is a great feeling and gaining respect will often outweigh many of the more tangible rewards people seek. Knowing that you will gain respect can be a great way of maintaining the motivation you need to keep making the effort to achieve your goals.

Passion

You are much more likely to stay motivated and indeed increase your motivation if you are doing an activity that you are passionate about. Having a passion for something gives you added qualities like more energy, enthusiasm, greater resilience, more focus and a stronger desire. You won't be able to feel passionate about all your goals and challenges, but for those where you can feel passionate, make sure you embrace them and make the most of those opportunities. It's a great feeling to achieve something you feel passionately about, so keep seeking those goals and challenges that get you excited and inspired.

'Never underestimate the power of passion.'
Eve Sawyer

Enjoyment

Some goals and challenges you will enjoy naturally whilst others may be much harder to achieve and find enjoyment in. But you will stay more motivated if you can find ways to enjoy the journey, so make an effort to smile, to laugh, to embrace the challenge and to remind yourself of all the benefits and positives that will come from the effort you are putting in. Look for ways to make the experience more enjoyable and focus as much as possible on the good aspects and the fun parts. The more you can enjoy the challenge the easier it will be to achieve your aims.

'Smile and laugh more than is considered normal!'

Confidence

The more confident you are the more likely you are to attempt new challenges and set new goals that will allow you to grow your confidence further and achieve more. The more you achieve then the more you want to do and your motivation will be higher as you realise how beneficial it is to achieve the goals. It is a wonderful positive cycle of confidence, motivation and achievement that leads to greater happiness. So, be part of that cycle and see how far you can go.

Self-belief

As with confidence, if you have belief in yourself you will look to achieve more and be more motivated to do this. Self-belief will also grow as a result of achieving things and being successful in your goals, so focus on your strengths, remind yourself of your qualities and skills and put in the effort to accomplish those goals. Your self-belief will keep increasing and as it does so you will be even more motivated to continue on that positive journey.

Being led by example

If you have a mentor, a role model, a coach, a boss or a friend who can help you with your goals through leading by example then you are more likely to be successful. Learning from them, taking good advice, being motivated by them, being encouraged by them and seeing how they would approach things and achieve the particular goals can be hugely beneficial. If you are lucky enough to have someone in this position then make the most of it, recognise it and embrace it. If you don't then see if there is a way to find someone who may be able to fit that role. It could be someone you don't know and who you never meet, but perhaps they have written a book; or information is available online that you can then use and be led by example in that sense.

Quotes

There are many quotes that have been written that can provide a great source of motivation. Throughout this book there are quotes that I like and feel are appropriate and many of these are very motivational. You may have others or you can go and look up 'motivational' quotes of which some are sure to inspire, motivate, generate desire, provide determination and reignite your passion.

Charitable aims

Your motivation and your desire to succeed are likely to increase if you know others are going to benefit as a result. So for example, if you were doing a physical challenge like running a marathon to raise money for a charity you feel strongly towards rather than running for yourself only, it is probable that you will find additional motivation to keep going when it gets tough. If you know that people have sponsored you, and many others will benefit as a result, then you are more likely to dig deeper, to try hard and to be even more motivated. So doing charity challenges is a great way to keep motivated and achieve great things not just for yourself but for others too, and attain an even greater sense of achievement.

'You make a living by what you get; you make a life by what you give.'
Sir Winston Churchill

Doing things in a team

For many personal goals and challenges you will find yourself on your own and often you will need to do things this way. However, if you have an opportunity to be part of a team then with the right people there can be a huge benefit to teamwork and feeling part of a team. You have other people who can support you, help you, guide you etc., but also you know that they are depending on you and you have additional responsibilities to them and not just for yourself. This can be very powerful in the right team, so look at opportunities to get involved in a team environment and your motivation and levels of achievement should rise.

Good weather

We have previously mentioned that bad weather can be a factor in poor motivation; however, good weather should be looked at in a very positive way. Make the most of good weather conditions like sunshine, long daylight hours, warm conditions etc. Get outdoors, make the most of it, use it to motivate yourself and then you can reap the benefits. We may get bad weather but we certainly also get good weather, so use it the right way and don't miss out on those opportunities to set goals and try new things. Vitamin D derived from the sun is also a great mood enhancer, and there's nothing better than exercising with the sun on your back!

Having clear goals and targets

The more defined and clearer your goals are, the more focused you can become and the less likely you are to be distracted. It may be necessary at times to be adaptable, and goals and targets may need to change, but if you are able to have clear goals and targets, preferably documented, then you will find it helps. It will help you stay motivated because it is clear what you want to do and why. It will also help you to explain to others, which can be helpful for advice, support and encouragement. And by having the clear goals you will be more efficient in achieving them.

'If you don't have goals, you can't accomplish anything.'

Sugar Ray Leonard

A good way to have clear goals is to use the acronym **SMART – Specific, Measurable, Attainable, Realistic and Timely**. Whenever you set yourself a goal or target, think about SMART because this way it is much more likely to be achieved.

Positive feedback

It is always nice to receive positive feedback from people and if you can get this along your journey it will help your motivation a great deal. The feedback could be directly related to a specific goal or challenge or it could be indirectly related and be a positive outcome as a result of the challenge. For example you may be training for a marathon and you have a training partner who gives you great feedback directly linked to your running progress or you could get feedback from people at work or family members who say you look great and have lots more energy, but that is an indirect piece of feedback. When you get positive feedback, make sure you take it on board and thank them and then use it to keep that motivation going.

Inspiring stories

A great way to get motivated is to read inspiring stories. There are so many amazing inspirational examples of courage, effort, dedication, hard work, sacrifice etc. that can really motivate you to achieve your goals. You can learn from their stories, understand better, prepare and plan more effectively, see how they did it and what was required and be in a better position to accomplish your goals as well as getting that added desire and motivation. There are a few examples in this book but I would encourage you to read books, go online, research, ask friends for examples of inspiring stories and see if they can inspire you to better things.

Time management

Managing your time, prioritising and being efficient are all going to be important in staying motivated and achieving your goals. The chances are you will have some constraints and pressures upon your time from work, family, children etc. So it is vital you manage your time well to allow yourself the time to focus on achieving your goals. Have a plan, write down a 'to-do' list, prioritise the list, keep checking back and updating the list and try to work out what is the best use of your time compared with how important those things are to you. And do not underestimate the importance of your personal goals.

Find the positives

We will always encounter obstacles, barriers, hurdles and negatives along our way through life and often these are out of our control. However, our attitude and the way we look at these issues can be within our control. We can take the positives out of a situation as long as we look for them because they are always there somewhere. This quotes sums it up perfectly:

'What is the difference between an obstacle and an opportunity? Our attitude towards it. Every opportunity has a difficulty and every difficulty has an opportunity.'

J Sidlow Baxter

Ticking things off a list

Usually with a particular goal or challenge you have set there will be various stages and milestones along the journey to achieving the final result. Try to break down the overall challenge into smaller stages, like bite-size pieces that not only become more manageable, but also allow you to be able to tick them off as you go. And celebrate these interim milestones in some way even if it's just giving yourself a pat on the back. If you are writing lists of things to be done then it's a great feeling to tick those things off the list and move forward. So, make sure you write lists and get ticking things off.

Preparation and planning

Many people who set themselves goals and challenges and then achieve them successfully will tell you that preparation and planning are key factors in their achievement. So if you prepare and plan well you are more likely to be successful and along the way you are more likely to stay motivated as you see a clearer path to that end goal. There is a saying that if you 'fail to prepare then prepare to fail' and if things don't go so well during the journey you will lose motivation. Therefore a really good way of maintaining your motivation is to take the time to plan and prepare sufficiently from the outset.

'One important key to success is self-confidence. A key to self-confidence is preparation.'

Arthur Ashe

Break it down into smaller goals

Often you will be faced with what seems a big problem or you want to achieve a big goal. You may find yourself thinking, at times, that it is just too big a problem or goal and it is not possible. This can lead to getting disheartened, feeling down or even giving up; however, a really good method to help with this is to look to break the goal down into smaller goals.

Each smaller goal will seem much more achievable and your confidence and motivation to succeed are likely to remain higher. A simple example of this is with running a marathon for the first time, especially if you are not a runner and haven't run more than a few miles previously. The big goal could become a big problem as running 26.2 miles is a very long way and could seem impossible. Yet, by breaking it down into smaller goals, with both the training and the actual marathon itself, it becomes more manageable and achievable. Aim to run 5 miles initially, then your target for a few weeks' time could be 10 miles, then a half-marathon the following month, followed by 20 miles the next month until you are ready for the full distance. The same principle can be applied on the day of the marathon by aiming to reach 5 miles, then 10 miles, then 15 and so on. This principle of breaking down big goals into smaller, more manageable goals can be applied to anything in life.

When you achieve each smaller goal on the way to the big goal, you will feel a sense of accomplishment and achievement that provides continued motivation and encouragement. Also, if you don't succeed at a smaller goal, the setback is smaller and you will be more likely to bounce back and go for it again sooner, so you can still reach the bigger goal.

Consider a task that you need or want to get done. Write it down here and then identify how it can be broken down into smaller goals.

'Nothing is particularly hard if you divide it into small jobs.'
Henry Ford

Energy

If you are tired it becomes easier to lose motivation, so if you can do things that help give you energy and you can prevent tiredness then you will stay more motivated. Getting adequate sleep and good-quality sleep is important, eating and drinking healthily will provide energy, worrying less, reducing stress and exercising more will all help towards benefiting your energy levels. In turn this will help your motivation and being motivated will also provide you with added energy.

Music

Music can be a great motivator. It can help give you energy, inspire you, make you feel happier and more positive and can take your mind off negative and unproductive issues. It can get you in the right frame of mind to tackle certain tasks and objectives too. Particularly for physical challenges and training towards those goals, music can really help. You might run faster and further, in the gym you might stay longer or lift more weights, in a circuit or spin class you might put more effort in and you might be motivated to take part in an activity as a result of the music. So, if you are searching for motivation, have a look through your music collection and see what happens.

The right surroundings

If you are struggling with motivation or getting too easily distracted by various other things then it may be you are in the wrong surroundings. For example, while writing this book there were times when I just couldn't focus and concentrate at my desk working from home. On a few occasions I would try alternative places, sometimes a coffee shop, sometimes a library and other times I would check myself into a hotel for a couple of days and set up my laptop. There were fewer distractions and I could concentrate better on the task in hand. Think about your surroundings and whether it is possible to change these, avoiding distractions so as to give you improved motivation to achieve the goals you want.

The right advice

Always seek the right advice whenever possible. If you are joining a gym for the first time, for example, make sure that you get the correct advice from a qualified instructor or experienced fitness person. There's no point, on your first day, in lifting huge weights or galloping along on the treadmill if you are not ready or fit enough yet to do so. Formalise a fitness plan, starting with a programme suited to your personal condition, aspirations and fitness levels. If you are unprepared or do things incorrectly then you are far more likely to suffer injuries, thus hampering your progress, knocking your confidence and reducing your motivation.

The right equipment

Depending on the particular challenge you are undertaking it may be vital to your success that you have the right equipment. Don't put yourself at risk of failing or lower your chances of success by not having the right equipment. For example, if you have set yourself a challenge of climbing Kilimanjaro, make sure you have appropriate footwear and clothing for the conditions. I have known people not reach the summit due to being too cold, because their jacket has not been good enough. There will be many examples in a wide range of different goals and challenges where your equipment is key, so make sure you give yourself the best chance of success by not compromising on the equipment you require. Seek expert advice if necessary or do the appropriate research.

Classes, groups, training partners

An effective way of keeping motivated and committing to something is to join up with other people in classes or groups, or find a training partner. Let's say you are trying to lose weight and get fitter but you have had a really bad day at work, feel tired and lacking motivation. There is a much higher chance that you will not exercise if your plan is to do something on your own and you are more likely to give up on that plan on that occasion. However, if you have committed to a class or group or have made arrangements to meet a training partner then you are far more likely still to go ahead. And guaranteed you will be pleased that you did and feel so much better for going. So think about how you can use classes, groups and other people to help keep you committed and motivated.

Commitment

Of course it is important to stay committed to a particular goal if you want to achieve it and we have seen that you are more likely to be committed if you involve other people, join in with groups and tell people about your plans. There are other methods you can use to maintain your commitment and motivation. Remind yourself of the rewards when you complete your goal, think about how you will feel and how that success will last and stay with you. Write down your goals, recognise your progress and visualise your success and the sense of achievement it will bring to you.

What has worked or not worked before

You can always learn from your past experiences and efforts and work out what has worked and what has not worked in order to give you the best chance of being successful in your current and future goals and challenges. Think about past successes and the reasons you have achieved them. Can you replicate these? Think about what hasn't worked so well before and see if you can eliminate those factors or change them in some way so that they do not become an issue again. You can gain motivation this way if you are struggling by looking at past experiences and using them to your advantage.

Tell people

If you tell people what your goals or challenges are then you are more likely to stay motivated, because you have effectively made a commitment and don't want to then back out of it. If you don't tell anyone then there is always a danger that you think 'well, nobody knows, so if I give up it doesn't matter'. It's important to tell the right people, those that will be supportive and helpful, but by telling them your plans you will have an added incentive that is likely to help maintain your motivation to succeed and complete the goal.

Prove people wrong

Some people find great motivation in wanting to prove people wrong. Perhaps those people are friends, family members, ex-partners, work colleagues, arch-enemies or even people in the media. It's a great feeling if someone says you cannot or won't be able to do something and you prove you can. You prove you are good enough, have the ability, have the fight, have the desire and strength to succeed and in some ways stick two fingers up at them. That can be very satisfying and a great way to motivate yourself in order to be successful.

'Sometimes I feel like giving up, then I remember I have a lot of #@##@#'s to prove wrong!'

Desire

One of the fundamental factors that will help you achieve your goals and stay motivated is having the desire to do it. You may not necessarily be passionate about something or enjoy it but you can still have the desire to make the effort and succeed in your goals. Passion is more natural, but desire can be developed and effectively manufactured from nothing. Think about all the reasons you want to succeed, think about your values, your hopes, your dreams. Think about the rewards and how they will outweigh the financial, physical, mental and emotional costs. Visualise the outcome and feel that desire within your body and mind and keep hold of it, as desire will keep you motivated through the difficult times.

Triumph over adversity

We all experience periods of adversity and suffer problems. But often this adversity can make you much stronger and bring out the best in you. Take the positives out of the negative situation and use the adversity to your advantage and to motivate you more, and you could be amazed by what can be achieved. In 1941, as Britain was in the darkest days of World War II, the British Prime Minister, Winston Churchill, told a generation of young people that *'these are great days – the greatest days our country has ever lived'*. He said this because he knew that it's when times are tough, when conditions are at their worst, that we can learn what we are truly capable of achieving.

Momentum

Sometimes you find yourself struggling to achieve your goals and you can find it very hard going, and other times you feel you are on a roll and things are going well. When you are going through a good spell then capitalise on it and build upon that positive momentum. Ride the wave, if you like. Momentum can be very powerful and if you feel focused, dedicated, determined and you can see yourself moving forward towards your goals then keep at it. Keep doing those same things and see how far it can take you.

Go to Fiji!

There is a really great story from Bear Grylls's book *A Survival Guide for Life* that is essentially about being able to motivate yourself to get on and achieve amazing things when necessary. Imagine you were offered an all-expenses-paid dream holiday, let's say a two-week break to Fiji, but it was leaving in three days' time. You have so much work to do and deadlines to meet in the next couple of weeks that you think there is no way you could go on that holiday. However, if you really put your mind to it, really focus, really make the effort, then you can organise yourself and work so hard on all the tasks and deadlines that what would normally take two weeks to achieve you can do in three days. If you want to go to Fiji then you will become motivated enough to do the necessary work. Give yourself that motivation and when you really want to get something done, tell yourself you want to go to Fiji and you will be amazed at what is actually possible.

Celebrate success

If you have worked hard, put in the effort and achieved results then you should recognise this and celebrate it. The success you have achieved and worked so hard for deserves to be celebrated. It could be smaller milestones along the journey that you celebrate and this in turn will keep you motivated or even motivate you more to keep going. Be proud of what you have done and what you are doing, praise yourself, recognise the achievement and celebrate your continued success. You will love that feeling and want more of it so this will keep you inspired and motivated.

Habit

Finally, there is a saying that we are creatures of habit, and I would agree. It is quite easy to fall into habitual behaviour. Usually this is seen as more of a negative and people talk about their bad habits. However, habits can be good and if you are doing things that become a good habit then that will be very beneficial. We have seen there are so many potential ways to help motivate yourself and thus help achieve things that if you do some of these and keep repeating them there is a strong chance they become more of a habit. You will start to do them without any particular conscious thought process. They will become second nature and the norm. And if you are doing these more and they are helping then you will be benefiting from all the knock-on effects. So look to make these positive actions, thoughts and behaviours a habit!

It always ends

There is a phrase that I often use to keep myself motivated that comes from the British mountaineer Kenton Cool. He has successfully climbed Mount Everest eleven times to date amongst his many achievements and when asked recently how he motivates himself when things get really tough, his reply was 'I just keep telling myself it always ends!'. You can apply this short phrase to any challenge, be it emotional, mental or physical. No matter how tough things get and how hard it is at the time, you have the knowledge that at some point it will end. The pain, the exhaustion, the cold, the hard times you are experiencing – whatever it is, it always ends. So on that next long run or mountain hike when you feel exhausted and your muscles are hurting, remind yourself that 'it always ends' and then you can relax and recover.

Now that was a long section with lots of tips and advice – I hope you agree! Were there any specific ones that really stood out for you? Or a few that really resonated with you? It is worth skimming back through them all and highlighting particular ones that made an impression on you and then writing them down and spending some extra time thinking about how they fit into your life, situation, plans and goals. **Use the box here to write these down and focus on them:**

Get rid of jealousy and be happy for others

Envy and jealousy

It is very easy to become jealous of someone and be envious of someone else's position or their particular circumstances. They have this or that, they look like that, they have money, they have the job, they have the car, they have the house, they have the partner etc. – a never-ending list of how someone else has it better than you. Now if that list was genuine and then you were able to use it in a motivational, aspirational, inspirational, positive way then being jealous might have some benefits.

However, it is much more likely that nothing positive will result from envy and jealousy. It will make you bitter, angry, upset and negative. You will be looking for excuses and reasons and blaming others as to why you don't have those things you want. You will become resentful and make false assumptions and poor judgements based upon envious and subjective emotions. Envy will have damaging and longer-term effects. It will eat you up, making you a jealous, bitter, negative person who will naturally dislike people, seek to blame others, and feel the whole world is against them. Well, life might not be fair, and you may have some bad luck and others some good luck, but envy and jealousy are very negative emotions. Nothing good can come of them and the sooner you get these damaging, destructive emotions out of your life the better.

If possible, whenever you feel yourself getting jealous, try to let that emotion go. Remind yourself that it is of no benefit to be feeling like that and having those thoughts. It is negative, non-productive and potentially harmful. You don't have to be pleased for them or have any emotion towards them, just ensure that you don't have any negative, jealous thoughts yourself that will affect you. Just let it go.

Once you have learned how to let it go, then you can feel in control of this harmful, negative emotion that is jealousy. It will no longer control you and have those damaging effects on you. You can rise above it and move forward with your life in a more positive way. Being in control of this then allows you, if you like, to turn other people's perceived good fortune and success into a more positive outlook for yourself.

Ask yourself why you perceive them to be fortunate and successful. Digging deeper into this area allows you to understand what you perceive success to be and allows you to think about what you want and what your aspirations might be. It may provide some goals, targets and ambitions and you can use this as motivation to start achieving some of these. However, along that journey you may also find that many of the things you were previously jealous about are not actually that important after all and your perception of fortune and success is different in reality.

The blame game

When something goes wrong or something doesn't go the way you would like it to then it is all too common for people to look for something or someone to blame. It's as if there must be blame attached to something or someone otherwise how could it have happened (or not happened). You may even blame yourself. But why do we do this? Why do we have to have someone or something to blame for anything that affects us in a negative, upsetting, or unfair way? We don't seem to be able to move on unless we have attached blame. There seems to be a real need for us to find the reason, or the excuse, for something and therefore blame can be given. So what is wrong with that?

There are two fundamental wrongs here in relation to the blame game. The first is to put blame on to something in a negative, unproductive way. There is little room for understanding or for learning from the experience. Saying it is his or her fault, or that was to blame, is a one-dimensional, emotive reaction from which no one benefits, even if it is true.

Secondly, have you ever heard the phrase 'shit happens'? Well, this is the real world we live in and in life shit does happen and often there is no person or no thing that is to blame. Things go wrong, negative stuff happens, things won't go according to plan or how you expect them to, and life will throw us a curveball. However, that does not mean there needs to be blame attached. You can accept the situation for what it is and move forward without all the negativity and unproductiveness of the blame game.

Assumptions and judgements

We spend so much of our time making assumptions and judgements both of events and of people, and much of this is necessary and natural. However, we often make unfair and incorrect assumptions and judgements, which can cause issues both to ourselves and to other people. You have heard the expression, 'don't judge a book by its cover' and you will be aware that you shouldn't make judgements without having all the facts or hearing both sides to the story, but that doesn't seem to stop us. In addition, when we are going through our own difficult times it seems that we tend to make even more assumptions, and make judgements that can be unhelpful, damaging and potentially destructive.

Making negative assumptions and judgements about events and people is increased and connected to being more paranoid and having lower self-esteem. This in turn causes more paranoia and concern that lowers self-esteem further and makes us think up even more negative and unhelpful assumptions and judgements. It is a vicious circle and difficult to get out of, unless you recognise what you may be doing and act upon that.

Try not to make assumptions or make judgements unless you are confident you have all the facts and a full understanding. Chances are you do not. Try to find out more or not think or worry about it at all. Do not feed your paranoia with negative possibilities and focus on unhelpful and unproductive scenarios. Instead, try focusing on things that will increase your self-esteem and reduce the paranoid thoughts and have a much more open mind. You might not be able to control what other people do and think, but you do have a choice over what you do and think.

'Before you assume, learn the facts. Before you judge, understand why.'

Comparisons

In a similar way to being envious and jealous of others we often create issues or make issues worse by comparing ourselves with other people, particularly people we know, whether that is family, friends, work colleagues or our peers. Many people spend much of their time comparing themselves to others, which is generally a very unproductive and negative thing to be doing. Only if the comparisons can help you focus, work harder, and inspire and motivate you to better things can it be beneficial. Usually, though, comparisons are made in a negative way.

Firstly, everybody is different, and in so many ways, therefore, you will never be able to compare like for like. Secondly, you are very unlikely to ever have all the facts and information, so comparisons are always built upon assumptions and judgements and we have previously mentioned the issues with that. Thirdly, comparisons nearly always make you focus on the things you don't have as opposed to the things you do have.

People have different abilities, different talents, different capabilities, all with varying strengths and weaknesses and mixed with different circumstances, timing and luck, so you just have to accept that like-for-like comparisons are not possible. Just because someone, in your opinion, has a better car than you or is better-looking or has more friends or has more money or has a bigger house or is smarter or is healthier or is more confident or has more luck etc., that does not really mean anything. It is your perception and your opinion and you do not know all the facts involved, and so what anyway? Focusing on those sorts of comparisons is damaging and is much more likely to reinforce negative attitudes and beliefs and be unproductive than do anything positive for you. Try comparing less and focusing more on what you have and the positive elements in your life rather than thinking or worrying about what other people have or don't have.

'Confidence isn't walking into a room thinking you're better than everyone, it's walking in not having to compare yourself to anyone at all.'

Be happy for others

We have talked about the negative problems associated with jealousy and envy and why it is so important for your own happiness and contentment to get rid of these emotions and thoughts from your life. However, there is another related problem that many people also have and that is the inability to be happy for others. Be honest and ask yourself if, when you hear about someone else's success, achievements, happiness or luck, do you feel happy for them or is there a sense of resentment, jealousy or bitterness?

If the answer consists of any combination of resentment, jealousy or bitterness then you have a problem that needs to be dealt with to help you have a happier life. Those emotions and thoughts are negative and unproductive and will do nothing for your own happiness and they will only keep you in a negative mindset.

However, if you can have a positive mindset, whereby when you hear about other people's good news, you can be happy for them then that helps maintain your own positive attitude, which we know is good for you in many ways. If you know them personally, then congratulate them, perhaps by a phone call, a text message or better still, in person. Even if you don't know them then you can still like a post on social media or offer a congratulatory message.

If you are not used to being happy for others, then at first, it might feel strange when you make the effort to be happy for others, but like with most things, it becomes easier and as your mindset is more positive it feels more natural and indeed helps you feel happier. Try it, make an effort to be happier for others, be pleased for their good news, their stroke of luck or good fortune, or as is more often the case, appreciate the hard work and effort they put in!

Learn to let things go

'You can't have a better tomorrow if you are thinking about yesterday all the time.'
Charles F Kettering

Our lives are defined so much from our past experiences and there is no getting away from that. All our thoughts, actions and beliefs are strongly influenced by what we have gone through in our lives and that can be both good and bad. However, too often we allow the bad things in our past to affect us in a detrimental way both in the present and the future. Additionally, we often find ourselves in situations where we keep pushing on, when the best thing for us is to stop and let things go. So in these two respects, it is really important to try, for our own happiness, to learn to let things go.

Let's start with the bad experiences from the past and how that may affect you. It could be difficulties from childhood like bullying, illness, not enough attention or love given or even abuse. It could be relationship issues, work problems, financial difficulties, people letting you down or other failures that have affected you. Some of these could be your fault in some way, though it is likely that most of these issues were not your fault and you had little or no control over them. It's important to recognise, remind yourself and accept that it was not your fault. And even if some bad experiences were down to you, that has happened and you can't turn back time. You can only influence the present and the future, so focus on that and not the past.

'My interest is in the future because I am going to spend the rest of my life there.'
Charles F Kettering

We often hear motivational quotes about never giving up or nothing is impossible and although they are well-intentioned, I often squirm a little as the reality is that sometimes you *should* give up and there are many things that *are* impossible! There is a big difference between giving up on something you should be doing and something you shouldn't.

A good analogy is climbing a mountain where you take an unknown route hoping to summit, but as you continue the terrain gets more difficult and perilous, but you push on regardless. You keep telling yourself not to give up but the rocks become increasingly challenging and dangerous and the weather gets worse. 'I can't give up,' you say to yourself again and again as the danger increases and your chances of summiting decrease. You soon find yourself in a very dangerous situation whereby you don't know where you are, you cannot summit and you don't know what to do. It's all well and good being determined and not wanting to give up but there will always be times when the best thing is to give up or to turn back. Live to fight another day, climb a different mountain, try something else and don't let pride, ego or stupidity mess up your life.

Have enough respect for yourself to walk away from something or someone if it is not good for you. Be honest with yourself and you will know what you should do. It might not be easy, it might feel like you have failed but it will be the right thing to do. Common examples include relationships, friends and work and they all play a huge role in our lives but there will be times when you need to walk away and let things go and have the courage to do so. I love the song and the lyrics to 'The Gambler' by Kenny Rogers. He might be talking about a card game but it really is a metaphor for life.

'You've got to know when to hold 'em, know when to fold 'em, know when to walk away and know when to run.'
'The Gambler', Kenny Rogers

It is also really important to realise that some things are just not possible. No matter how hard we try, how much work we do or effort we put in, there will always be things that we will be unable to do. Setting yourself unachievable goals that you think are achievable will more than likely end in disappointment and potentially despair and depression.

Be careful in setting goals. Don't get me wrong, I am a huge believer in goal-setting, having aspirations, pushing yourself, dreaming big etc., but there has to be a sense of reality. Don't waste your life on the impossible but instead make the possible happen. I love this quote I came up with several years ago when I had to accept something I wanted to do was not possible. It didn't stop me dreaming and thinking about what is possible but my admitting to myself something I wanted was not achievable gave me a sense of relief and closure and the disappointment soon left me.

'Not everything is possible; but possibility is everything.'

ACHIEVEMENT

'Do something today that your future self will thank you for!'
– Sean Patrick Flanery

What is achievement?

The formal definition of 'Achievement' is '***a thing done successfully with effort, skill or courage'.***

Here are a few more descriptions of achievement from other people I have asked:

- Achievement is overcoming a set of obstacles to reach an end goal. What is classed as achievement is personal and very different to each individual.
- Achievement is something you know will make a positive difference to someone/thing, be it yourself or others. It's a feeling that makes you proud, satisfied and rewarded.
- An achievement is completing something you've set your mind to. The fact that you've had a goal, stuck to it and had a positive end result.
- Achievement is doing something successfully with maximum effort, courage or skill. It is something important to yourself, which has meaning and makes you feel proud of yourself.
- Achievement is being the very best that you can be in the circumstances that you are in.
- Achievement is completing your own goals and the passing of personal hurdles.

Why is achievement so important?

Ultimately the reason that achievement is important is that it makes us happier. We all want to be happy and one of the best ways to improve our happiness is through achievement. This can come in many different ways and on many different levels and will vary from person to person. There are many types of achievement, many reasons for setting particular goals and achieving them, many resulting factors and positive knock-on effects too.

If you don't achieve things or look to achieve things then what are you actually doing with your life? Clearly it depends upon your perception of what an achievement is, but having goals, targets, aims, ambitions, challenges to work towards and then complete is a fundamental part of living and being alive. Hundreds of thousands of years ago a big achievement might be for a group of people to go out and hunt animals so they could feed their families and community. There was a goal and a purpose and it took effort, skill and courage but the rewards were very clear. Nowadays it is less of a challenge and achievement to feed your family. So we need other challenges in our lives where we can have that purpose and get that sense of achievement.

There are so many things you could do, so many goals and challenges to achieve. Many will form part of your normal life, such as work-related challenges or bringing up your children, but take time to think about what else you would like to achieve. Write down potential goals, ambitions, targets etc. and think about how important they are to you. Think about how you could achieve them, what help you would need, how long it might take, what resources you require and very importantly, how good you will feel once they are achieved.

Below are some of the areas that highlight why achievement is so important, so read through and think about how they could apply to you and the goals you want to achieve.

Your health

Achievement is a key ingredient in the recipe for happiness, confidence and success. If you are achieving things you are also likely to be healthier, with both your physical and mental health being improved. As we have mentioned before your health is very important and it should never be taken for granted. You have a responsibility to take care of your health, and achievement through your life will definitely be a part of taking responsibility.

In addition, if you are achieving things and your health is improved as a result this will have a positive knock-on effect with other people in your life. The healthier you are the more you can do, the more you will inspire others and the more positive an influence you will be to those around you, impacting on their health and happiness in a good way.

Confidence

There is no doubt that feeling and being more confident is a good thing and most people would like to be and feel more confident. There is also no doubt that achieving things and succeeding in your goals will increase your confidence. In fact achievement is definitely one of the best ways to increase confidence. So if you want to improve your confidence you should be focusing on achievements and if you need a reason to achieve things then it could be as simple as increasing your confidence, which in turn will make you happier.

The more confident you feel then the more likely you are to achieve more goals and set yourself different challenges so it becomes a great momentum for ongoing happiness. On the other side of the coin, the less confident you feel, the less you will achieve so it creates a negative spiral. Make sure you do those things that will help you to increase your confidence and increase your ability to achieve things and keep practising the techniques and take the advice, as the rewards will be worth the effort.

'Achievement is a sure way to increase confidence.'

Purpose and Fulfilment

It is fundamental to human nature that we need to have purpose and fulfilment in our lives. There needs to be a reason for living and we need to be doing things with purpose and achieving goals otherwise we find ourselves merely existing. The likely consequence of not having purpose and fulfilment is a negative spiral that can lead to depression, low confidence, low self-esteem, low self-worth, lack of energy, negative thinking and essentially unhappiness.

A good example to show this is when people retire. For most people who have worked hard for several decades, retirement is something to look forward to. They can enjoy the additional time, they can relax, they don't have the pressure and hassle of work any more and they can go and do things they want to do. That all sounds great, yet many people once they retire become unhappy and depressed and this is usually because they lose that purpose and fulfilment they used to get from working. Getting up each day and going to work gives you a purpose and contact with people, which is important and whether you recognise it or not there is a level of fulfilment. If this goes and is not replaced by other activities and goals then it can become an issue.

Achievement can provide purpose and fulfilment in a number of ways. Setting goals, targets and challenges for yourself complements our instinctive human nature and they become a key ingredient in that recipe for success and happiness.

Respect

There are many measures of what brings us happiness and contentment in our lives and it will vary from person to person. Some of these are given to us, some happen by chance and some are earned by our behaviour and actions. It is great to feel respected by others because you have to earn respect and it demonstrates you have done things or achieved things that have made people notice, and their respect has been given as an acknowledgment of your efforts.

There is, of course, also self-respect. This is even more important to have. Earning respect for yourself from what you do and how you do it is key to your own confidence, your self-esteem and being at peace with yourself. By setting goals and challenges, making the effort, working hard and achieving these targets is a sure way to building and maintaining that self-respect.

Pride and Satisfaction

Feeling satisfied and proud of yourself is a wonderful feeling to experience. If you set yourself some goals and you achieve them, no matter how big or small they are, then there will be a level of satisfaction. You had a goal and a purpose and you fulfilled that. Furthermore, you will feel a sense of pride and typically the bigger the achievement the larger that feeling of pride is.

Being proud of yourself can boost your confidence, improve self-esteem and provide contentment and happiness. It's a warm inner feeling that usually shows on the outside by your behaviour and actions: feeling more positive, smiling more, enjoying things, getting involved, being more social and believing in yourself and what you can achieve.

Pride will make you want to do more positive things and this in turn will create more opportunities, allowing you to set new goals and achieve more and provide that sense of satisfaction. Don't underestimate the power of pride and the benefits that it brings and therefore don't forget how important achievement is in creating pride.

'Pain is transitory; pride endures forever.'

Strength

The more you achieve the stronger you will become physically, mentally and emotionally. You will be able to draw upon your experiences, learn from the process, develop skills, tools and techniques that work for you and basically become a stronger person as a result.

There is no reason why you wouldn't want to become a stronger person and one of the best ways to achieve this is through achievement. The stronger you are the better you will be at dealing with life's challenges that will inevitably occur. You will develop more resilience, more courage, more determination, more physical power and a greater confidence, which are all attributes you would want and will also further your ability to achieve greater successes.

If you don't set goals or challenges in life then you won't give yourself the opportunity to grow stronger and develop as a person. So look to build that strength, slowly but surely, and the results will come.

Praise and recognition

Achievement will usually bring many benefits that will often attract praise and recognition from others. Sometimes obtaining that praise and recognition is the primary reason for the effort or the main factor in keeping you motivated, so to receive it is very satisfying. Perhaps you get rewarded with something tangible like a prize, a certificate or a medal. Maybe it's a round of applause, a bonus payment, a big hug or a thank-you card. There are many ways in which your achievements can be praised and recognised and it is important to take this in, embrace it, remember it and use it to inspire and motivate you for future achievements.

It is also important to recognise and praise the achievements yourself. Take time to acknowledge what you have done and, if appropriate, reward yourself in some way as you deserve it given your efforts, sacrifices, determination and commitment and make sure you encourage, praise and recognise other people's achievements too.

Financial reward

In our society, for better or worse, money plays an important role and most people would like to earn more or have more money. If particular goals or challenges lead to a financial gain then not only can this be a big motivator but it can also be a strong reason for having the goal. Achieving a particular challenge that you have set which then brings financial benefits so you can support your family and provide more security is a great feeling. Achieving goals may also bring indirect financial rewards. For example, if you are able to demonstrate certain qualities and strengths through non-work activities that can be highlighted on a CV and discussed in an interview process, this may aid you in obtaining a better job with greater financial rewards.

Brain and body chemistry

There can be direct physiological benefits associated with achievement where certain hormones are released and certain neurotransmitters in our brains are regulated, and levels can increase. For example, your adrenaline levels can be raised, making you more alert, more focused, more positive and more energised. You may find that through achievement your serotonin levels increase, leading to a better mood, with you feeling more content and generally happier.

You may have heard about the 'runner's high' with the release of endorphins when you exercise that makes you feel alive and very positive. These feelings are great and can be generated by your own actions. There can be a positive cycle, whereby the more you achieve the more positive physiological and neurological benefits you receive, which then lead to you being more motivated to achieve more and so on. The increased neurotransmitters and release of positive hormones make you feel so much better both physically and mentally, so if you can improve this by setting goals and achieving those goals successfully then go ahead and do it.

Effort and reward equation

Another reason why achievement is so good is that most of the time there is quite a fair equation that takes place between effort and reward. Basically you will get rewarded in some way for your efforts and the more effort the greater the reward. That is satisfying to know and should help you with motivation and also setting goals in the first place.

Of course, there are times when efforts go unrewarded or the level of reward seems far less than the effort you put in but generally speaking the equation is reasonably fair. You shouldn't expect to get rewarded without any effort and if you do then the reward is not actually as good and doesn't mean as much. However, if you have worked hard, made sacrifices and really made an effort then the rewards that come from this are much greater, are much more satisfying and mean much more to you.

Inspire and motivate others

A final area to look at in this section about why achievement is important is the effect it can have in a positive way on other people. No doubt there are certain people and particular achievements that have inspired and motivated you. We looked earlier at a few inspirational stories and those achievements and it is great that they can then help others to achieve things and ultimately be happier.

Although your particular goals and challenges may be quite individual they have the potential to inspire and motivate others. Perhaps those other people are friends, family members or work colleagues who draw inspiration from your achievements or perhaps they are total strangers who see or hear about what you are doing. Isn't it wonderful that you could be doing something that not only benefits yourself but has the power to inspire and motivate others too?

Someone might follow your example and be motivated by seeing the results you have achieved or they may think that something is now possible whereas before they may have believed it to be unattainable. One of the best ways to get motivated is to gain inspiration from other people and their stories and achievements so it is therefore very important that people do achieve things; why not be one of those people who others look to for their motivation? Wouldn't it be great if someone told you that you are an inspiration!

'I want to inspire people. I want someone to look at me and say "Because of you I didn't give up".'

How to be successful and achieve things

Everyone is different and you need to find out what works best for you in terms of what you want to achieve and how you define success and then how best you go about it. However, in this section below I have highlighted what I believe to be important factors and proven methods that should help. In addition, it is a reality that if you are more confident and more motivated then you will achieve more, so with the information provided in the previous sections and with time and effort improving those, then you will achieve more and be more successful.

Goal setting

You would like to achieve something and be successful in that endeavour or particular goal? How do you ensure you are successful, or rather, how do you ensure you give yourself the best opportunity to succeed? There are a number of generic steps that should apply to most goals that you may set yourself, so if you follow them and apply these goal-setting steps you will give yourself the best chance of success and achieving your goals.

1. Setting goals for the right reasons

It is important to understand why you want to achieve a certain goal and what the reasons are behind that ambition. Are they the right reasons? Take some time to consider how the goal will improve your life and benefit you and others in the process. Why do you wish to take on that particular goal or challenge? What are you hoping to get out of it? Is the goal realistic and achievable? Will the success of achieving the goal outweigh the time, effort, cost, sacrifice, pain etc.?

If you are comfortable and clear that the goal is being set for the right reasons then let's move on and go for it!

2. Planning, preparation and commitment

You now have a goal that you have set and want to achieve so you need to plan and prepare effectively. Think about the time it will take, the costs involved, the people you may need help, input and support from, the equipment you may need, the skills you may require and anything else that could be a factor. Write down all of these and draw up a plan that is realistic and also measurable where possible so you can track progress.

Take your time planning and preparing because so much of your success will be built from these solid foundations you have set and which you can build from. Then commit fully to that plan!

3. Belief, passion and enjoyment

You need to have confidence and belief in your goal and that you can achieve it. The more passionate you can become about the goal and the more you can enjoy the journey the more likely you are to be successful. You have set a goal, you have planned and prepared and you are committed to it, so you should believe in yourself and what you are doing. The reasons for making the effort are clear and the rewards far outweigh the sacrifice, so you should feel that energy and belief growing even stronger.

With every day and every effort made the goal will get closer to being achieved, so keep believing, keep passionate and enjoy the journey!

4. The right people

Some goals will be very individual and only you will be involved, but in most cases the goals and challenges will involve other people. It is so important to involve the right people. Choose the ones that believe in you and your goal, those with the appropriate skills, knowledge, expertise, experience and enthusiasm, the people who you can rely on and who will understand and support you. That is easier said than done so take your time, don't compromise yourself and remember quality is nearly always better than quantity.

If you find the right people then that can be a huge factor in your success, so make sure you appreciate them and treat them well too!

5. Desire and determination

It is likely that on any goal or challenge you will experience a few knock-backs and negative moments when things don't go as you wish. There will also be times potentially when you question yourself and want to give up. As long as you still believe in the goal for all the right reasons then you need to get through those difficult times and setbacks. If you have the desire and the determination then you will be strong enough and resilient enough to keep going. Occasionally you may need to change plans or give up on the goal if you no longer believe it is the best thing to do; however, take your time on deciding this as you don't want to regret any decision.

If you suffer setbacks or criticism or things are tougher than you imagined then use those experiences to add fuel to your fire, making your desire and determination even stronger!

6. Keep practising

Very few goals will be achieved quickly and if they are then they probably weren't particularly impressive goals. You will need to have patience and perseverance and, of course, you will need to keep practising. Practise the skills, the training, the effort, the visualisation, the thought processes etc. so that you keep improving and developing. Whatever the goal, it is likely that the more practice you put in towards achieving it, the higher your chances of success.

The more you practise the better you will become and the easier it will seem so that you can then push yourself even more to achieve even greater things!

7. Celebrate achievements and steps towards them

As you move towards your goal you should be able to measure yourself against your plans and see your improvements and how far you have come. It is not just about the achievement of the end goal, it is also about the journey and all the successful steps along the way. They should be recognised and celebrated. This should encourage and motivate you to keep going towards your goal and also help you enjoy the process.

Remember the more you enjoy it the more likely you are to succeed, so celebrate those achievements along the way as each step is getting you closer to your end goal!

8. The end goal

Never lose sight of the end goal, your reasons for setting the challenge and all the positive benefits that will result from your achievement. As we have seen it is important to break the journey down, take it step by step and be patient and take your time. However, the end goal is the prize and the main motivational factor in most challenges. Visualise the achievement and the success and remind yourself of all the positives.

Once you have achieved your goal you will always have it. Nobody can take it away and it can provide strength, confidence, inspiration and motivation for future goals!

'Be ambitious – think big and take calculated risks.'

Other factors

Enthusiasm – Be enthusiastic in what you are doing as it will make a big difference to your chances of success. Many things are out of your control, but you can choose to be enthusiastic about your attitude and what you are doing. Enthusiasm can be inspiring and infectious in a good way as well as being a positive emotion and behaviour.

Courage – We all have some fears we face in life and times when we are scared and where we need to be brave. But being brave isn't about not feeling scared. Real courage is all about overcoming your fears. As this quote from Mark Twain says, '**Courage is resistance to fear, mastery of fear – not absence of fear.**' And of course there is also the well-known saying, '**Fortune favours the brave!**'

Give extra – Often the difference between ordinary and extraordinary is just that willingness to give that little bit extra. It may sound a little corny but it is true. If you can put in just a little more time, push a little bit harder, focus even more intently, keep going that little bit longer, then it will make a difference and it could make all the difference.

Travel light – Don't be afraid in life and during challenges to travel light. Excess baggage and bad, unnecessary equipment will slow you down, making it much harder for you. Remember that the most important equipment and resource is always your attitude.

Sacrifices – See sacrifice and suffering as a type of fuel that powers you towards your goals. It's never easy to make sacrifices and to suffer, especially when it hurts, physically and mentally, but choose the option that will make you proud. If you sacrifice and suffer in order to succeed you will experience a feeling of genuine pride that is very hard to beat.

Integrity – It is so important to maintain your values and integrity. Keep your word, honour your promises and see your commitments through. That integrity and those values you demonstrate speak volumes and will attract the right people who can help you succeed in your goals; if you lose your integrity and compromise your values then the challenges and any achievements will be less worthy.

Train hard – Treat training with respect and put in the effort as that will be where most of the difference is made. The will to win means nothing without the will to train and a quote from Muhammad Ali states, **'I hated every minute of training, but I said, don't quit. Suffer now and live the rest of your life as a champion.'**

It's your life – Remember that you should be living your life, not someone else's, and stop trying to do everything for everyone and be everyone for everything. This quote sums it up, **'I don't know the key to success, but the key to failure is to try to please everyone.'**

John Naber story

A true story that is a great example of breaking down a seemingly unachievable goal into a realistic and manageable target is from the American swimmer, John Naber. He participated in the 1972 Munich Olympics as part of the American relay squad and although he helped them reach the final he was not one of the final four members who won gold. He left those games very disappointed and vowed that at the next Olympics he would make the final team and come away with an Olympic gold medal. His discipline was the 100m backstroke and he wanted not only to be part of the country's relay team but to compete in the individual event too.

He researched what would be needed to win the gold medal at the next Olympics by looking back at history, past records, progress made over the years and the ability of his main competitors, and predicted that to win the 100m backstroke race in 1976 he would have to swim it in 55.5 seconds. The major problem he had was that his personal best in the event was 59.5 seconds, a full four seconds slower, which was a huge amount and seemingly unachievable. He thought he had no chance and his dream of Olympic success was over.

He then began to look at things differently and realised that although an improvement of four seconds was a massive margin, he didn't have to achieve that tomorrow, next week, next month or even next year. He had nearly four years to achieve this, so that meant a one-second improvement per year. Training for approximately ten months a year, that was then only one-tenth of a second improvement per month. With on average thirty days in a month that was just an improvement of $1/300^{th}$ of a second per day and with four hours' training per day just a $1/1200^{th}$ second improvement per training session. It takes $5/1200^{th}$ second to blink and now he only had to improve $1/1200^{th}$ second each time he trained. He now believed that was achievable.

With these more realistic and manageable targets each week, month and year he trained with confidence and, most importantly, belief. At the 1976 Summer Olympics in Montreal, up against the reigning champion and world record holders, John Naber went on to win the gold medal and he did it in a time of 55.49 seconds!

'The greatest danger for most of us is not that our aim is too high and we miss it, but that it is too low and we reach it.'

Michelangelo

Be more active

'Action is a great restorer and builder of confidence.'
– Norman Vincent Peale

There are so many reasons why being more active is good for you, yet it is important to understand why so that you are more likely to be active. So often, we feel tired, we lack energy, our motivation is low, we have so much to do, we feel stressed and it can feel a real struggle to be active when all we want to do is relax on the sofa and put our feet up! And sometimes, relaxing, resting and putting our feet up is the best thing to do. However, being more active will most likely give you more energy, increase your motivation, make you feel more positive, improve your fitness and health, help you to achieve more and will build your confidence.

It is important that you get a balance and don't try to do too much, but being more active and more productive will feel good as you get more done, become healthier, feel more energised and gain a sense of pride, which in turn will boost your positivity, create opportunities for you – and you will be amazed by what you can do and how it helps you to be happier.

Move more

Of course I would recommend exercising regularly, going to the gym, doing classes, running, cycling, walking, doing team sports etc., and we will come on to those, but you can make huge improvements and gain significant benefits just by moving more each day. You can easily burn off an additional 25-300 calories each day just by making a concerted effort to move about more, and this extra movement will soon add up to some noticeable improvements to your body.

- Park your car further away from the office, train station, supermarket etc., and walk that bit extra.

- Use the stairs wherever possible rather than the lift or escalator.
- Get up and walk around the office or go up and down your stairs at home on a regular basis.
- When nobody is looking, get up and dance, wave your arms about or do some shadow-boxing!
- When sitting down at home or at work, wave your legs up and down.

Human evolution – born to be active

There is so much evidence in all different forms that indicates we are healthier and happier if we exercise, and exercise can come in so many ways and just about everyone can find some activity they can do and hopefully enjoy. However, often people associate exercise with running and most people in modern times unfortunately don't run and are horrified at the thought! They are too unfit, overweight, not used to running, don't find it appealing, can't get motivated, can't run very far or very fast, and it is simply easier not to bother. And why should we bother when we have cars, trains, buses, bikes etc., for transport? We no longer have to go hunting for food as we just drive, or occasionally walk, to the shops. We are very rarely put in positions of danger where we have to run from something or towards something for our safety. There just isn't the need to run, so why bother?

Well, another way to look at this, apart from everything that will be said on the benefits, is to show how humans are natural athletes and we are literally born to run. Unlike any other animal on the planet we have evolved into the most intelligent, superior species. That has happened for a number of reasons that include the very important ability to run like no other creature.

There are so many features and unique qualities to the human body that seem to show clearly that we were born to run. For example we have an Achilles tendon that is only needed for running. Why do we have this unless we were designed to run? And why do we have arches on our feet with small toes to allow us to run, whereas chimps and monkeys don't have Achilles tendons or arches, just flat feet with very long toes designed for walking and climbing. We have a nuchal ligament in the back of our neck to support our head and balance it that is only needed for running. Dogs, cats and horses have a nuchal ligament to help them run but again chimps and monkeys do not. Humans also have big bums that are very helpful for running yet have no benefit for walking. Next time you see a chimp, look at how small their bums are compared to those of humans.

A further unique feature of humans is our lack of a tail. No other running animal or two-legged creature has no tail. The way we balance while at speed is the added combination of the nuchal ligament in the neck and the fact that our heads are heavy compared to other animals. This heavy weight on the top of our upright position provides support and balance, allowing us to move at speeds and for long distances without wasting too much energy.

We are upright creatures with features that are only found on our four-legged animal friends who are renowned for their running and speed. Yet, unlike horses, dogs, cats, deer etc., our breathing is not directly in relation to our movement. Watch a leopard run across the African plains and the breathing is directly related to their strides – as their legs stretch out, their lungs open and when their legs close together with the stride, their lungs contract like bellows. So while their breathing is matched with their running stride, humans' breathing is different as we typically will do at least two strides to one breath.

Another very important feature and strong advantage is the number of sweat glands we have. No other creature has as many and can sweat so much. This ability to sweat helps us to keep cool for much longer.

So although many animals can run faster than us they cannot sustain that for very long before they overheat and have to stop or slow down significantly. If you take a dog out on a hot day and they run and run, they will eventually just stop, and this will be much earlier than a fit and healthy human.

'Don't ask me why I run... Ask yourself why you don't.'

There is an annual horse versus man race over a fifty-mile distance. Most people would never dream that a human could beat a horse in a running race, yet most years the humans come out victorious. Animals just don't have the endurance that humans have because they cannot sweat and keep cool for long periods. Humans have the best air-cooled engine of any animal and are able to run for hours at a time if necessary. Something else that might surprise you is that humans have a longer running stride than a horse. If you record and slow down the footage of a horse then you'll see that each leg has a relatively small stride and the energy required to run fast with all four legs that way is significantly more than a human. So whereas a horse can go at a much faster rate for about ten minutes they soon slow down to a slower pace than a strong long-distance human runner.

Unlike most sports and activities running is age-friendly. What I mean by that is that humans can go on running to what would be considered very old age without losing much of their ability compared to their younger years. A large study was done on marathon runners and it was shown that if you take the average best times for someone at nineteen years of age and compare those across the age range, then humans reach their peak in terms of running ability after eight years at the age of twenty-seven. The subsequent decline in ability is significantly less than the time it took to reach the peak. Not until age sixty-four does a human's ability fall back to their ability at age nineteen. So eight years of improving and thirty-seven years of gradual decline. So in many ways this shows that 'you don't stop running because you get old – you get old because you stop running!'

Something else to consider and observe on the opposite end of the scale is how young children are so naturally active. They can seemingly go for hours playing, running, jumping and being active, and it looks so normal and natural. The reason is that it is natural and normal for children to be active and enjoy being active and this should be encouraged for as long as possible. Before computer games and televisions, children would spend much of their time actively playing, using up energy, running about and enjoying the natural freedom and benefits it brings.

As children get older they generally become less physically active and that seems to be due to three main reasons. Firstly, there are so many alternatives these days to what we can do, with computers, games and television, and it is easier to encourage children to do these as it requires less effort and is easier for parents to manage. Secondly, as a consequence of many factors, including poor diet and nutrition, worsening sleep habits, more stress, and health and safety issues, children lack motivation, are more tired, and have fewer opportunities to play, exercise, do sports and be physically active. Finally, we do not appreciate the benefits of exercise or are not fully aware of the health risks and consequences of not exercising due to a lack of education, training, and learning.

If children were encouraged to keep being active, like they do so well naturally as young children, then more of them would benefit and be healthier and happier. If there was more education, more opportunities, more emphasis placed on exercise and activity, it would benefit us all.

'Your body can stand almost anything;
it's your mind that you have to convince.'

Stop sitting

The act of sitting can literally make your bum bigger! Research found through using MRI scans of muscle tissue that sitting around for long periods of time could put pressure on cells and cause the body to produce fifty per cent more fat than it would normally. It suggests that when force is applied to a specific area of the body for an extended time, it causes fat tissue to expand.

Also, as you sit down, the electrical activity in your leg muscles shuts off and the number of calories you burn falls significantly, plus enzyme production that helps break down fat drops by up to ninety per cent. Additionally your good cholesterol levels drop and all these effects combined really have a very negative effect on your health. Even if you do a lot of other exercise, you are in some danger if you sit around for long periods of time.

Another reason for not sitting around for long periods is that your blood sugar and insulin levels will spike to potentially dangerous levels, but getting up and moving about regularly will counterbalance this.

So try sitting around for less time and take frequent breaks where you get up and walk around for a minute or two. Get into the habit of sitting at your desk for no more than twenty minutes before some kind of initiated action. Stand up, move your legs, squat down, or do a little jiggle! If you can break the habit of sitting for long periods of time it will make a big difference in many ways and you will soon get into a much better habit of being an 'active' sitter.

'Let exercise be your stress reliever, not food.'

Commit to exercise

Too often we say we will do some exercise and then we come up with an excuse not to do it. Let's stop those excuses, and one of the best ways is to commit to the exercise and activity. What I mean is sign up to a class, join a running group, arrange to meet a friend, set a specific time to do exercise and stick to it.

You need to plan, make the time, and then commit. You will always be glad you did it afterwards even if you didn't feel like it beforehand. And, of course, you know it will get you results and help improve your body.

'I don't* find *the time to exercise... I* make *the time to exercise.'

Physiological and mental health benefits of exercise

***'To keep the body in good health is a duty... otherwise we shall not be able to keep our mind strong and clear.'* - Buddha**

EFFECTS ON THE BRAIN CHEMISTRY

We all know that exercise is good for us and can improve our health and make us feel better, yet most of us don't actually know why. The main reason is that exercise makes our brains function at their best. Physical activity is crucial to the way we think and feel and plays a significant role in regulating and improving our neurotransmitters and bolstering our brains' infrastructure. The brain responds like most muscles do by growing with use and withering with inactivity. The neurons in the brain connect to each other like leaves on branches, and exercise causes those branches to grow and bloom with new buds, so enhancing and improving our brain function.

The brain is, of course, very complex and much of what goes on is still not really understood. However, it is known that many of our thoughts, behaviours and emotions are controlled by chemicals in the brain called neurotransmitters and the key neurotransmitters are:

Serotonin – responsible for mood, anxiousness, self-esteem, and impulsive and compulsive behaviour.

Beta-endorphin – responsible for modulating emotional and physical pain. It contributes to feelings of self-esteem, euphoria and emotional confidence.

Norepinephrine – affects arousal, alertness, attention and mood.

Dopamine – vital to movement, attention, cognition, motivation, pleasure (and addiction).

Ideally, we would all have regulated and optimal levels of these neurotransmitters so we feel happy, well balanced, confident, and our thoughts, behaviours and emotions are how we would like them to be and seen as 'normal.' However, for many people this is not the case and their neurotransmitters are lower than optimal and poorly regulated leading to a range of emotional and mental health issues that also affect physical health.

Exercise and physical activity is a fantastic way of helping to elevate and regulate these chemicals and make us happier, more alert, less stressed, less anxious, more balanced, less reactionary etc. Our brains will respond very quickly to exercise, and positive results and outcomes can be seen immediately, as well as continued and sustained benefits. Our brains are so important and should be given the respect and attention that is necessary, and the good news is that exercise can be incredibly effective for our brains and therefore our overall health and well-being. Do not underestimate what exercise can do for your brain!

'Exercise is a wonder drug that hasn't been bottled.'

Different types of exercise

There is such a huge range of physical activity that can be classed as exercise and there really is something for everyone. Take time to think about all the different potential exercise options there are, and how they could become part of your life, or at least whether you are willing to try them out.

Here are some examples of different types of exercise, and I am sure you can think of some more!

Walking, Hiking, Running, Climbing, Swimming, Cycling, Pilates, Yoga, Dancing, Aerobics, Zumba, Martial Arts, Football, Rugby, Cricket, Tennis, Squash, Badminton, Softball, Lacrosse, Hockey, Netball, Basketball, Golf, Athletics, Circuit training, Horse Riding, Sailing, Rowing, Skating, Skiing, Sex, Weightlifting, Gymnastics, Bowling, Gardening, Housework and many more!

'Only exercise on the days you want to feel happy!'

What do you enjoy or what did you enjoy in the past?

There are so many options when it comes to exercise and activities, and it is worth taking time to really think about what you want to do, why you want to do it and how you will do it. Think about any activities you have previously done and enjoyed. Can you do this again? Why did you enjoy it? Think about it in a positive way and make plans to take these up again.

Are you able to do more of the activities you enjoy? Perhaps you can do them more regularly or with different groups or in different places? Chat to friends, family members and work colleagues about what they do, or would like to do, and see if anything grabs your interest and enthusiasm.

The more you enjoy something the more likely you are to do it, to make the effort and to stick with it. So if you know you enjoy something then start with that, but if you can't think of anything, or there are limited options, then think carefully about all the other possibilities and give some a try. You won't know whether you like it or not until you try, and the more different options you have the better.

Recently I started going to street-dance classes, which are great fun and also a great workout. I do a lot of exercise and activities, but I was thinking about what else I could do or try that might be of interest and my mind turned to dancing. I have never danced before, except when I was a lot younger at discos and clubs and usually after several drinks, though I used to enjoy dancing on these occasions. So, enjoying music and the idea of dancing, I quickly came across a local group after mentioning the idea to a friend and it has been great and something I will continue with. It uses a few different muscle groups from my usual activities, it is a lot of fun, burns lots of calories, and with a great bunch of people.

What would you like to try?

Life should be enjoyable, you should try and do things that make you smile, that you want to do and that are good for you as much as is possible and practical. Life is also about living and not just existing, so it is important to try things and find out what you like and don't like. When it comes to exercise, sport and physical activities there are so many possibilities and things you could try.

So think about what you would like to try if you could. Take away all the potential barriers like being scared, not knowing how to do something, not having the money, not having the time, or having nobody to try it with. What does the list look like if there are no barriers?

Now think about how good it is not to have regrets, to step out of your comfort zone every now and then, to scare yourself from time to time, and to really feel alive. Think about investing money in your health and happiness, rather than just the cost of something, and think about investing time into your life for these activities, as the rewards are more than worth it.

It may be something completely new or an activity that requires a lot of skill to learn and if so then be patient and build up slowly over time. Believe that you can do it and the time and dedication will be rewarded.

Try researching on the Internet for the opportunities, people, groups, organisations and clubs that may be helpful in your quest. Speak to friends, family and colleagues for ideas, advice, encouragement and motivation, and try those things that appeal to you. If you start doing activities that are enjoyable, fun, rewarding and healthy then that is a fantastic place to be and to continue doing. If you find a passion, make new friends, become fitter and healthier, increase your confidence and everything else those activities can bring then you will be so much happier and really be living your life. So go for it!

Gyms, groups, clubs, boot camps and sports clubs

Most people will have access to a wide range of exercise, sporting and physical activity opportunities close to where they live, which can be very beneficial. Although factors such as cost, equipment, timing, work patterns and family life practicalities can all be factors, there is usually something for everybody if you look into the options.

Gyms and health clubs are very common and although they can vary in types of membership, facilities, costs and opening times, there are often many choices, including pay as you go, off-peak membership, 24-hour access and special deals throughout the year. Gyms and health clubs can provide an excellent environment to train, attend classes, meet new people, go with friends or family, go on your own, get expert advice and guidance, free inductions and much more.

Outdoor boot camps have become increasingly popular in recent years, and most towns and cities will have a wide range of options for all abilities. Being outdoors in the fresh air with a range of exercises and other people can be a fun, enjoyable and social experience as well as being a great form of exercise.

There are also many clubs you can join or go along to with a wide range of activities and a variety of different sports, including running, hiking, sailing, rowing, martial arts, dance, keep fit etc. Often they are very low-cost and sometimes free. Again they can be social, fun and cater for a wide range of abilities. Talk to friends and work colleagues about what they know, or do a quick Internet search and you will undoubtedly find many options available.

All these opportunities are there for you and can provide huge benefits if you participate, invest your time and commit to them. You have nothing to lose and so much to gain in so many ways!

Events and challenges

Have you ever participated in a big physical activity event of any kind? Whether it be a 5k race, a half marathon or full marathon, a cycling race, a swimming gala, an organised charity walk, an outdoor obstacle course, a charity mountain climb, or anything that combines exercise with lots of people?

If you have you know how great they can be! The atmosphere, the excitement, the nerves, the camaraderie, the encouragement, the support and the sense of achievement and pride they can produce. If not then you have missed out and I would encourage you to try it. Apart from all the benefits you get from training for the event, you can benefit so much more from the experience and your achievement.

Have a think about what you could do or would want to try and aim for. Even if you have never done anything before, for nearly everyone it is possible to run a five-kilometre race with a few months' training if you build up slowly and sensibly. Plus it's not about the winning or the times; it is about the participation, the experience and the achievement. There is also the opportunity to do it for a good cause, which is likely to further enhance the experience and achievement by gaining extra support and encouragement and by helping others in the process.

Stepometers, pedometers, apps and gadgets

A very simple, yet very effective little device you can buy is a stepometer or pedometer-type gadget that effectively measures how many steps you take over a period of time. They can be wristbands, watches, small clip-on devices or even necklaces. Once you start using it you can quickly find out how many 'steps' you do per day and then start setting particular targets to increase this.

For example, it may be that on average in your first week you do around

6,000 steps per day. However, if you set a target of 8,000 steps and are able to monitor it regularly you will find that you can fairly easily increase your activity to reach that new target. Then once you have reached this you can aim for even more, say 10,000 steps per day on average. This doesn't mean you have to do loads more exercise, as a few extra steps here and there, a slightly longer walk at lunchtime, a bit more moving around at work etc., quickly adds up to a lot more steps.

You can then get a rough idea of the extra calories burned, which will add up significantly to your weekly count. Having the monitor and setting targets is a great, yet simple way to be more active and of course you can always have a competition with your partner, family member, or friend to motivate you even more. Also, many of these devices have additional features and you are able to download all the information quickly and easily to help record your efforts.

In a recent study, it showed the average American only reached 5,117 steps per day whilst the average Australian reached a more impressive 9,695 steps per day, almost double the rate. This perhaps also helps explain why Australia's obesity rate is sixteen per cent, whilst in the United States it is thirty-four per cent.

There are, of course, so many different gadgets and apps nowadays that can be used and be very helpful and effective. Personally, I use a Fitbit watch that is synced to my phone to give me lots of data, including, steps, floors, heart rate, calories used, sleep patterns and more. And although it cost around £80, I feel it has been a good investment, providing additional motivation as well as useful information.

'Exercise doesn't get in the way of my life...
it adds to the quality of my life.'

Active at work and home

When you are awake you will most likely spend the vast majority of your time either at work or at home. If you think about how many hours per day you are either at work or at home then there is a huge opportunity to be more active in these places, which could have significant benefits. Of course there are many practicalities that may restrict you but there will undoubtedly be things you can do to increase your activity levels and therefore improve your health.

Depending on your work environment and the obvious practicalities, think about how you can be more active. Walking up the stairs rather than using a lift, parking your car further away and walking, getting up from your desk and walking around the office regularly, going for a walk outside at lunchtime or other breaks, moving your legs under the desk etc. Over the course of a week you could easily burn an additional 1,000 calories by just intentionally being a bit more active at work and that can make a big difference with hardly any real effort.

There could be some exercise classes, running clubs, or walking groups already organised or you could help set some up. Chat to other people at work who may also want to increase their activity levels and see what options there are.

At home there are lots of exercises and activities you can do specifically, as well as more generally. You could do some specific workouts at home, maybe using a DVD or music that could be either dancing, aerobic workouts, exercise bike, weights, yoga, or weight-bearing exercises. These could be for as little as five minutes at a time to a full hour. There are lots of equipment pieces that could further aid your activities.

In general terms, it is more about intentionally being a little more active by getting up from the sofa or chair more often, walking up and down the stairs more, waving your arms about (when no one is looking!), moving your legs up and down while sitting etc. There is a lot you can do whilst at home that increases your activity levels, burns calories, increases your fitness, and in turn improves your health. Plus the more you do the easier it becomes and the more long term the benefits.

***'Those who think they have no time for exercise will sooner or later have to find time for illness.'* – Edward Stanley**

Eat well – you are what you eat

'Let your food be your medicine and your medicine be your food.'
Hippocrates

Something that we all do on a daily basis is eat and most of us don't appreciate what a huge influence what we eat has on our lives. Both our physical and mental health are massively affected, both positively and negatively, by what we eat. And to a very large extent we have control over what we eat and therefore we can make a huge difference to our physical and mental health by focusing on this area.

Most people do not eat very healthily. The majority of the population is overweight and we all know that a poor diet, eating unhealthy food and too much food is the main reason for this and our physical health suffers as a result. Obesity, diabetes, high blood pressure, heart conditions etc., are all known issues that are significantly influenced by what we eat. These physical conditions are also likely to make us less active and thus compound the issues further. We can, however, improve our physical health substantially by eating well and although not easy, the benefits from a healthy diet are so huge that we should all make more effort.

In addition and often overlooked, is the effect that eating well can have on our mental health. The food we eat plays a massive role, both directly and indirectly, in how we feel. Eating well can lift our mood, give us energy, help us sleep better, increase our confidence and self-esteem and so many more benefits, and on the contrary, an unhealthy diet can have the opposite effect. The saying, 'you are what you eat' is very true and hopefully some of the information below will help you to improve your diet and to understand how eating well (or not) can really have an impact on your life.

Cut out the sugar

One of the biggest modern issues that causes health problems, obesity, lethargy and other conditions is our huge consumption of sugar and in many cases our addiction to sugar. It is very likely that you have far too much sugar and you will make a massive positive difference to your life if you cut out the sugar or at least reduce it to a recommended level. Please read the section further on about sugar.

From now on pay really close attention to how much sugar you are having on a daily basis in your food and drink intake. Wherever possible make a note of how much you are having by checking labels. **Typically one teaspoon = 4g of sugar.**

You should not be having more than 30g of sugar per day (7 ½ teaspoons)... this is the new World Health Organisation's recommendation, announced in 2015.

How much sugar do you have? Look at the table below and then also fill in the spaces with your own examples of foods and drink you typically have and find out how much sugar is in there. Then calculate on average how much sugar you would typically have each day.

Food or drink example	Approx amount of sugar	Food or drink example	Approx amount of sugar
Low fat yogurt	20 g		
Low fat muffin or cake	35g		
Tin of baked beans	20g		
330ml can of Coke	35g		
Bowl of Frosties cereal	20g		
500ml bottle of vitamin water	15g		
A Mars bar	20g		
Caramel Frappuccino	45g		
Sweet & sour chicken ready meal	22g		
Can of tomato soup	15g		

Approximately how much sugar would you have per day? __________

Sugar addiction in more detail

Over the last few decades there has been a huge increase in sugar consumption that has led to both an increase in weight and many people becoming sugar addicts. There are two main reasons why there has been such a massive increase in sugar in our foods and drinks: firstly, sugar is very cheap and secondly, it can be very addictive. Food and drink manufacturers benefit enormously from these two reasons and therefore sugar is prevalent in so much of what we eat and drink. To increase sales and profits it is therefore in manufacturers' interests to use sugar in vast quantities and in so many products. Very few will care about our health and there is no incentive to reduce or cut out the huge sugar content.

Governments have seemingly only recently realised the significant health issues and costs to public health as a result of sugar, yet there is little they can do or will do. Unless serious action is taken to educate people and companies, together with tougher regulations then the problem will only continue and worsen.

Because sugar is a cheap ingredient for manufacturers and is addictive, so many of the special offers, bargains, deals, fun adverts, colourful attractive packaging etc., are on these products. People love a bargain, are enticed by the advertising and promotions, and of course for many people they love the taste, the feeling, as well as many being addicted.

In many ways sugar should be seen as a drug because of its addictive qualities and the effect it has. Many people have strong cravings for a sugar 'hit' and they need their 'fix' and once they have had the sugar they get a short-term 'high' that makes them feel good. However, like most drugs this soon wears off and can leave people feeling worse, lacking energy and with a lowering of mood. They have a blood sugar high followed by a blood sugar low.

Sugar is often associated with giving us energy, and indeed sugar in its various formats can provide us quickly and effectively with the glucose energy our bodies and organs, including the brain, need. However, if that glucose and energy is not used then the body will store it and put it into our 'reserves' for later use. Most people will not use the energy at the time or in the future and these 'reserves' build up by converting to fat stored on our body and around our internal organs. Of course, over time this builds and builds while our sugar intake continues.

Another factor is that in many of the 'low-fat' products seen in our shops and on our shelves today, there is a huge amount of sugar. Manufacturers can fool people with apparently healthy 'low-fat' products yet they contain large amounts of sugar, which inevitably turns into fat on our bodies. So be very careful and aware and look closely at the food labelling and ingredients on both foods and drinks. The recommended daily amount of sugar is now no more than 30g and that works out at 7½ teaspoons per day. So try to calculate your sugar intake from foods and drinks and remember that unless you are using that energy then it will end up in your body being stored as fat.

Your blood sugar and what happens to your body

When you have sugar your blood sugar levels increase and for a short period you feel great. You have effectively had your 'fix' and you feel a short-term 'high' with increased energy and a satisfying feel-good feeling in both body and mind. Your body needs some sugar but nearly all of us have far too much and your body cannot deal very well with such an overload. What typically happens after the initial high is that your blood sugar levels then dip, often dramatically, with unhelpful consequences to both body and mind. Not only can your body not use all the energy and metabolise the sugar, thus storing it as fat reserves, but with the fall in blood sugar levels you can experience the following effects:

LOW BLOOD SUGAR EFFECTS

- Tired all the time
- Tired for no reason
- Restless, can't keep still
- Confused
- Having trouble remembering
- Having trouble concentrating
- Easily frustrated
- More irritable than usual
- Getting angry unexpectedly

Some advice to help you cut down on sugar intake

The two most important things with regard to sugar intake are firstly, to realise the damaging effects of consuming too much sugar and secondly, to monitor what you are eating and drinking closely to see how much sugar you are actually having. Here is my advice on how to reduce sugar intake and some practical suggestions that you can try out:

- **Become an expert on looking at food and drink labels to identify how much sugar you consume**
- **Set yourself a target of no more than 30g per day of sugar and praise yourself every time you go under this**
- **Write a food diary highlighting how much sugar you have per day**
- **Stop adding sugar to drinks like coffee and tea**
- **Do not give in to peer pressure with cakes, biscuits, sweets, chocolate etc., offered to you**
- **Do not keep high sugar food and drink in the house – avoid the temptation**
- **Stop 'rewarding' yourself with sugary food and drinks**

How to deal with the sugar cravings

Firstly, your cravings for sugar WILL decrease as you consume less sugar. It WILL become easier if you stick to the low-sugar plan and the cravings will go! However, in the meantime or if you do have any cravings then try the following tips:

- Go and brush your teeth
- Chew sugar-free gum
- Have a cup of hot water with lemon or a green tea
- Go for a hot shower or bath
- Do a quick high intensity workout
- Do some meditation

- Eat a healthy snack – e.g. some vegetables!
- Write down a list of future goals, or why you want to be healthy
- Visualise your brain with the 'bad' message demanding sugar and the 'good' message defeating the baddie!

'The key to healthy eating? Avoid any food that has a TV commercial!'

Eat loads of vegetables and salad

As we have just seen, pretty much all salads and vegetables are under the 'full' calorie category and you can basically eat as many vegetables and as much salad as you can. They are so beneficial in so many ways and the higher the percentage of your daily diet they are the better off you will be.

Vegetables and salads should be seen as the REAL comfort foods, with nutrients that actually improve your resilience to stress. Eating vegetables helps replenish your magnesium and vitamin C, which can be depleted by stress. Vegetables also provide you with omega-3 fats and B vitamins, proven to help reduce anxiety and depression. The vitamin K in veggies helps reduce inflammation in your body, which stress can aggravate.

Green leafy vegetables, such as kale and spinach, are loaded with magnesium, which helps balance your cortisol, one of your 'stress hormones'. Magnesium and potassium relax blood vessels, helping keep your blood pressure low. Magnesium also plays an important role in calcium absorption, helping you maintain good muscle and nerve function and a healthy immune system. Low magnesium levels have been linked with anxiety disorders and migraines, both of which are typically aggravated by stress.

Avocados are one of the best stress-busting foods you can eat, replete with potassium, glutathione, healthy fats and more foliate than any other fruit. Foliate is extremely important for your brain. Asparagus, for example, is also rich in foliate.

Fresh vegetables are also great when it comes to bone health. They provide forms of calcium, magnesium, silica and a host of other minerals that work synergistically to build strong, healthy bones. One of the fat-soluble vitamins playing a critical role in bone health is vitamin K2, as its primary function is to move calcium into the proper areas (teeth and bones). Vitamin K2 also helps direct calcium away from areas where it can cause problems, such as your arteries and soft tissues.

One of the best sources of vitamin K2 is fermented vegetables made with a special starter culture designed to optimise this nutrient. Fennel is also very good for your bones, particularly the seeds. Research has shown that eating the seeds of the fennel plant has a beneficial effect on bone mineral density, as well as bone mineral content. Researchers found that fennel seeds show potential in preventing bone loss in postmenopausal osteoporosis.

Most vegetables and salads are naturally low in fat and calories, so are great for losing weight. None have cholesterol (though be careful of sauces, dressings or seasonings as they may add fat, contain sugar, calories, or cholesterol). Vegetables are important sources of many nutrients, including potassium, dietary fibre, foliate (folic acid), vitamin A and vitamin C. Vitamin A keeps eyes and skin healthy and helps to protect against infections. Vitamin C helps heal cuts and wounds and keeps teeth and gums healthy and aids in iron absorption.

Diets rich in potassium may help to maintain healthy blood pressure. Vegetable sources of potassium include sweet potatoes, white potatoes, white beans, tomato products (paste, sauce and juice), beet greens, soybeans, lima beans, spinach, lentils and kidney beans.

Dietary fibre from vegetables, as part of an overall healthy diet, helps reduce blood cholesterol levels and may lower the risk of heart disease.

Fibre is important for proper bowel function. It helps reduce constipation and diverticulitis. Fibre-containing foods, such as vegetables, help provide a feeling of fullness with fewer calories.

A great way to eat more vegetables is to store them in your freezer so you always have some to hand and they don't go off or out of date very quickly. Frozen vegetables will keep their nutritional value and are just as good as fresh vegetables and are easy to prepare from frozen. So stock up that freezer with healthy vegetables!

Some practical tips!

- **Start adding more vegetables to your meals and by so doing take out the carbs like pasta, rice and chips.**
- **Eat raw vegetables as snacks rather than chocolate or cereal bars.**

Experiment with trying out new salads and vegetables – there are so many out there!

- **Try growing your own vegetables and salads – cheaper, healthier, more rewarding and you're more likely to eat more!**
- **Fill your freezer with vegetables so you always have plenty available to eat.**
- **Buy some Tupperware boxes and fill them with chopped vegetables and salads and keep them in the fridge so they are always available.**

'If you keep good food in your fridge, you will eat good food.'

Ignore the dream snatchers

Sadly there will always be people who are jealous and envious of others, who will be unsupportive, put people down, be negative, talk behind people's backs and hope people fail in their goals and dreams rather than wanting them to succeed.

These people we can call the 'dream snatchers' and wherever possible you need to get rid of them and not have them in your life. Inevitably, though, there will be some and whatever their reasons are they will of course have a negative effect on you – if you let them.

So, try to get rid of them, but if not you have to ignore them. You are better than them. Be a 'dream supporter' yourself, embrace the other supporters and ignore the snatchers!

As you go through this programme and your body improves and your confidence increases, there will hopefully be lots of people who notice and are supportive and encouraging. They will say nice comments, ask you how you are doing it, be interested in and proud of what you are doing for yourself. Sadly, you may come across a few people who are jealous and not supportive – ignore them and be better than them!

However, it is not just related to this programme where you should take note. With life in general you should have dreams and set goals for yourself. Have things to look forward to and to aim for and be confident in your decisions and targets. In turn, as you achieve these goals your confidence will increase further and you will do even more great things in your life.

You can get a lot of confidence, hope and inspiration from other people and their stories. There are so many examples of inspiration, triumph over adversity, the will to succeed, belief in dreams etc., that can be used to motivate you and in turn help build your confidence, and can be a help in ignoring the dream snatchers!

'No one can make you feel inferior without your consent.'

Eleanor Roosevelt

Here is a great example of a real-life inspirational story:

Dick Fosbury was an American high jumper who changed his sport forever by adopting, at the time, a completely new technique to high jumping that became known as the 'Fosbury Flop'. For the last few decades every single one of the world's top high jumpers has used the technique he created, but in 1968 at the Mexico Olympics he was the only person who did. He was a relatively unknown athlete who came away with an Olympic gold medal and new Olympic high-jump record.

He always enjoyed sport and was a reasonable athlete during school, competing in a few high-jump competitions at local school level without huge success. Back in the 1960s there were two main techniques that high jumpers used – the straddle and the scissors technique. With the straddle you effectively threw yourself over the bar head first on your front. With the scissors you went over the bar in an upright seated position. Dick Fosbury's athletics coach tried to encourage the straddle technique, whilst Dick Fosbury himself preferred the scissors technique, yet with both of these he was well below the standards of a state champion, let alone a national champion.

Fosbury then started to play about with his technique and found that if he went over the bar leaning backwards, in a scissor-kick style but then flipping his backside over the bar he was able to clear heights he had not previously been able to. Despite his coach being dismissive of this new technique and trying to encourage him to work on the straddle, Dick Fosbury persevered with his own technique and his confidence and belief in this grew.

His personal best kept improving and people started to take notice, yet at the same time people and spectators were laughing at this strange new way of high jumping. A newspaper termed it the 'Fosbury Flop' and the name stuck. There were so many people within the sport and the public and media outside the sport who put him down and were the dream snatchers. However, he continued to make huge improvements and simply ignored all the people who rubbished him or laughed at him, and in 1968 he qualified as one of three members of the USA team for the Mexico Olympics. He was still a relatively unknown athlete and was seen more as a circus act than a gold medal prospect. He won the event and became Olympic champion. People took notice and jumpers took notice. He changed history and within a few Olympic Games every high jumper had adopted his technique.

He found his own way and methods, grew in confidence, and stuck to his beliefs. He ignored the dream snatchers. His confidence grew because he was getting results and he knew it was working. So find what works for you and if you are getting results, keep going. Have the confidence to keep going with what you believe in if it works for you and ignore those who don't.

'Stay away from negative people.
***They have a problem for every solution.'* – Albert Einstein**

Stop the excuses

We all know people who say they are going to do something but don't, who talk the talk but don't walk the walk, who put things off and who always have an excuse. DO NOT BE ONE OF THESE PEOPLE!!

Stop the excuses – be honest with yourself and give yourself a metaphorical slap round the face whenever you find yourself being one of these people. Nobody is perfect and we all have blips or bad days, but make sure you do not consistently make excuses for not doing those things that are going to be good for you and improve your life. You want to be happier and healthier, and making excuses will not help that.

Sometimes there are very legitimate reasons for not being able to do something, but you will know the difference between a reason and an excuse. Get rid of the excuses and keep kicking them to touch whenever they try and creep into your life – as with most things the more you practise it the easier it becomes and you will find yourself stopping the excuses and instead doing so many more productive and beneficial things.

'Excuses will always be there for you. Opportunity won't.'

Importance of lifestyle and habits

Humans are very habitual creatures and that means that they are good at forming habits. Unfortunately, far too many of those habits are not good for us. These bad habits become part of our life and are a big factor in many people leading unhealthy lifestyles. And we know that unhealthy lifestyles will cause issues with our physical, mental and emotional health.

Often the problems build gradually and because they materialise as a result of our everyday habits and normal lifestyle we tend not to really notice and therefore we don't place much emphasis on them. For example, putting on weight gradually, perhaps a stone over a three-month period. If this happened overnight we would certainly notice it and be shocked and horrified, yet because it happens over time, gradually, we usually ignore it. The same can be said with a build-up of stress.

So it is really important to be self-aware and notice our lifestyle and habits and the effects they have on us and our health. It will be much easier than you think to form good, healthy habits because we love habits and are good at them, so once we start them we are good at maintaining them. These good habits will then form the basis of a healthy lifestyle and it will become much more normal than you could imagine. But you have to start and keep going until they become good habits.

Practise, practise, practise

There are many 'quick wins' to improving your body and increasing your health and happiness; however, some of these will not last unless you keep doing them. More importantly, if you really want to sustain your body improvement and be happier for the long term then it really is a case of practise, practise, practise! As the saying goes, 'the more you practise, the better you get' and this is very true with body improvement.

Let's look at an analogy to highlight the point. If you had low confidence and wanted to be much more confident you could relate this to being a slow, unfit runner who wishes to be able to run a marathon. You are capable of running a marathon but not straight away. It will take several months to build up the strength, the fitness, the stamina, the belief etc., and the same applies to confidence. You need to practise over time and slowly but surely you will achieve the goal.

You will also need to look at many factors. With running a marathon you will be looking at other factors than just running, such as footwear, other clothing, your nutrition, hydration, other types of training, training partners, motivation, advice, encouragement and much more. In order to go from being a poor runner to being a good runner there are many elements to work on, many factors to consider, and it will take time and a lot of practice; otherwise you won't be able to do it.

It is very likely that along the journey of going from being a novice runner to being able to complete a marathon you will have some setbacks. Perhaps an injury, a couple of bad training days, an illness that prevents you running, or a lack of belief that you can do it. The same is likely to happen as you go along your journey of building your confidence, but you need to keep patient and keep believing and you will keep moving forward. Don't let the setbacks deter you from your goal. Keep practising!

Reflect and reassess

Along your body-improvement journey there will be times when you need to reflect upon how you are doing and what you have achieved so far. It is always important to reflect and take a step back at times for various reasons. Perhaps you need to see how well you have done, recognise this and be proud of that. Potentially you may need to think if you are really committed to the programme and if not then make adjustments.

By taking a bit of time to reflect on your progress you can see more clearly the positives and any potential negatives. Sometimes it is not easy to see the progress as you only see small changes daily, yet over several weeks they add up to big changes. Embrace the positives and look to build upon these even further, and if there are any negatives then understand and learn from them to then turn them into positives.

It may be the case that you need to reassess some things. That is OK because you need to work out what works and what doesn't work for you. It is far better to stop, reflect, understand, and reassess and then make the right, positive changes that will work, rather than keep going with something that isn't working.

Good people around you

It is important in life to have good people, and the right people, around you. That is often very difficult to achieve, but if you make the effort towards getting the good people in your life then it is more likely to happen. With regard to the body-improvement programme it is also very important to have good people around you.

Most of the effort and work must come from you, but in terms of encouragement, support, motivation and other help then having good people around you will be a big advantage. Ignore, dismiss, or get rid of anyone who is not supportive of you and may be a negative influence on your goals. Don't let them and their issues become a reason for you not to reach the goals you want to achieve. Often it is jealousy that is the reason behind any negativity and that is their problem and not yours.

With the good people you should ensure you appreciate them and thank them and be good back to them. Utilise them and benefit from them, but make sure you give back and are one of the good people around them too.

Final thoughts

I really hope this book has been informative and beneficial to you. Confidence is so important to a happier and healthier life and this can be improved in many ways but especially through increased motivation and achievement and the more confident you are the more you will be motivated and will achieve. So please keep using this book and reread whenever you need to, as often some of the things mentioned need to be read more than once. This is your book to look at and refer to whenever you want.

I would love to hear from you with any comments or feedback, and hopefully hear how the book has helped you. Please feel free to contact me via email: info@climbyourmountain.org

Best wishes

Charlie Wardle
Founder of Climb Your Mountain (CYM)

More from the Charity

Climb Your Mountain (CYM) was set up as a charity in 2008 with the aim of helping anyone who is going through a difficult time in their life by helping them to climb their own personal mountain. It is for anybody, any age, any background, and recognises that stress, depression, low confidence, health issues, associated conditions and lack of general well-being can be damaging and can affect anybody for many different reasons.

The charity has two main focuses. Firstly, there is an emphasis on using physical exercise and activities as a way of dealing with, managing, preventing and treating issues. There is a wide range of benefits to physical exercise and activities, yet it is often hard to motivate yourself, especially when you are feeling low. Also, many people are not aware of the huge benefits that physical exercise and activities can have on your mental health and well-being, as well as your physical health. So the charity provides opportunities as well as encouragement and motivation for people to do more exercise and take part in more physical activities. We have organised hundreds of free walks, hikes, runs, climbs and cycle rides across the country, in a friendly and safe environment. Anyone can participate and people are there to benefit from enjoying the activities, meeting new people, seeing new places and becoming healthier and happier.

The second focus is on education and providing information and knowledge for people about physical and mental health and overall well-being. CYM offers free educational talks, courses and workshops that cover a wide range of topics including stress and depression (symptoms, causes, prevention, management and treatment), anxiety, brain chemistry, food and mood, benefits of exercise, confidence and self-esteem, motivation and barriers to well-being. There are also the self-help books that expand on the course content and can reach more people, offering practical help and advice, so they are in a better position to help themselves and to be able to help others.

Please visit the website **www.climbyourmountain.org** for more information and to get in touch. If you know of any groups, organisations or companies that would be interested in a talk or course, then get in touch.

How you can help others

We rely heavily on donations and sponsorship to fund our services, including providing these free books. If you can help us in any way or would like to volunteer or be involved, then you can help many other people. Please get in touch!

We also organise overseas treks and challenges as fundraising events for the charity with trips such as climbing Kilimanjaro, the Everest Base Camp trek, Pyrenees Thousand Lakes trek, Mount Toubkal, Great Wall of China trek, the Inca Trail and others. So again, if interested, get in touch!

Please email info@climbyourmountain.org

Or go to the website www.climbyourmountain.org